SPORTS AND ATHLETICS PREPARATION, PERFORMANCE, AND PSYCHOLOGY

THE MENTAL EDGE IN BOXING

SPORTS AND ATHLETICS PREPARATION, PERFORMANCE, AND PSYCHOLOGY

Additional books in this series can be found on Nova's website
under the Series tab.

Additional E-books in this series can be found on Nova's website
under the E-books tab

SPORTS AND ATHLETICS PREPARATION, PERFORMANCE, AND PSYCHOLOGY

THE MENTAL EDGE IN BOXING

ROBERT J. SCHINKE

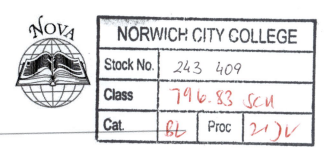

Nova Science Publishers, Inc.
New York

LIBRARY OF CONGRESS CATALOGING-IN-PUBLICATION DATA

Schinke, Robert J.
The mental edge in boxing / Robert J. Schinke.
p. cm.
Includes index.
ISBN 978-1-61324-296-4 (hardcover)
1. Boxing--Psychological aspects. I. Title.
GV1133.S37 2011
796.83--dc22

2011011440

Published by Nova Science Publishers, Inc. □ + New York

DEDICATION

I dedicate this book to my wife Erin and our two children, Harrison and Pierce. As well, I need to acknowledge a member of my working team, who serves as the head of my second family: Marc Ramsay. Finally, much love and respect goes out to my longest-term athlete, JP. JP: thanks for pushing me forward in my practical thinking – we academics often become far too caught up in our well-insulated ivory towers. You are an athlete ahead of your time. Appreciation and respect also goes to Stefan Larouche and Yvon Michel for welcoming me into the professional boxing ranks as part of their team many years ago.

ABOUT THE AUTHOR

Robert Schinke, a Tenured Full Professor and federal government endowed Canada Research Chair in Multicultural Sport and Physical Activity, holds a masters in sport psychology, a doctorate in Educational Leadership and a post-doctoral year in Positive Psychology. His research interests span cultural sport psychology, resilience, and adaptation. A former Canadian Equestrian Team Member and Pan American Games Team member as an athlete, Robert's innovative research with elite athletes has been funded by the Social Sciences and Humanities Research Council of Canada, the Canadian Foundation for Innovation, and the Canadian Institute for Health Research, among other funding sources. His publishing, upon which he was awarded the 2008 Canadian Sport Science Research Award, has been accepted into the International Journal of Sport and Exercise Psychology, The Sport Psychologist, the Journal of Sport and Social Issues, the Journal of Clinical Sport Psychology, the Journal of Applied Sport Psychology, Quest, and the Journal of Physical Activity and Health, among many other internationally respected publishing outlets. He has authored three applied sport psychology books, each released in multiple languages, and six edited textbooks about sport psychology, with international contributors from North America, South America, Europe, Africa, Asia, and Oceana. Schinke is the Editor of Athletic Insight and he has guest co-edited an installment of the International Journal of Sport and Exercise Psychology, devoted to the intersection of culture and sport and exercise psychology. Most recently, Robert is guest editing the Journal of Clinical Sport Psychology and the Journal of Sport and Social Issues concurrently, while also writing two new books pertaining to the sport psychology and athlete cultural identity intersection. Robert lives in Sudbury, Ontario, Canada, with his wife Erin and sons Harrison and Pierce. He also travels extensively to work with professional athletes and their coaching and managerial staff.

ABOUT THIS BOOK

Within this book, Dr. Robert Schinke shares with you, the reader, how to mentally sharpen aspects of your boxing performance. Robert has worked with several notable boxers, including amateur and professional world champions and also lineal Ring World Champions, for almost twenty years. Regardless of whether you are a boxer, coach, or a member of a developing or elite boxer's support system, you will find this book to be informative and extremely practical. The topics featured as part of this book include how to train effectively, how to develop athlete self-confidence and mental toughness, how to profile an opponent, and how to carry out a detailed plan from the moment you have identified your opponent through to success and beyond. Read this book and see for yourself how to be even more systematic in terms of the mental edge of boxing performance. This book is a must read for boxing enthusiasts, and also those immersed in combative sports such as mixed martial arts, kickboxing, Thai boxing, karate and jujitsu.

CONTENTS

Chapter 1

INTRODUCTION

Three weeks ago one of my professional boxing clients became a unified world champion, with his bout featured on HBO World Championship Boxing. Before the bout, odds makers in Las Vegas bet 4-1 in favor of my client's opponent as that athlete was on the pound for pound top 10 listing of most every expert who evaluates professional boxers. Though some believe that statistics and probabilities are indicators of future performance, bet makers included, numbers alone do not get to the essence of athlete performance, in boxing. Boxing is a mental game where a less accomplished boxer can outshine a more experienced and a more talented opponent through intelligence, preparation, the coordination of human resources, and sound decisions. For the more focused athlete, talent and focus meet regularly with opportunity, and the result is always profound and positive.

Over the last 12 years, I have worked with professional boxers, including several world champions, from North America, South America, Africa, and Europe. My first world champion achieved his objectives within six months of collaborative work, followed closely by a second world champion one month later. Both of these clients during my formative experiences were not believers in sport psychology and mental training. Both athletes held previous experiences working with sport psychology consultants. In one case, the athlete regarded sport psychology as esoteric and a waste of his time. Even with the athlete not having to pay personally for the service, he anticipated that such services were irrelevant and also without practical basis. Luckily, by the time I met the aforementioned client, he was willing to try almost anything, having lost several previous world title attempts, the most recent by knockout. Try he did, and with sport psychology services linked to high quality coaching, he became a world champion, and then went on to defend his title multiple times.

The second early client had a different experience with sport psychology consultation. He was a foreign athlete with an extensive and prolific amateur sport background. During his early years in elite amateur sport, he was told he had to work with his national team's sport psychologist. The athlete found the services of the consultant not only without pertinence, but also not trustworthy. It seemed that from the athlete's view, the consultant was sharing personal information with the athlete's coaching staff in order to gain favor with the national team's formally appointed staff. As you might imagine, the services that people like me provide are bound by ethical guidelines, including confidentiality. Those guidelines are an integral part of how I work, and most important, if one's approach is ethical, a strong relationship is forged with boxers and their supporting cast.

When I began working with both athletes during the same year, my biggest challenge was to earn trust and overcome well-founded distrust and fear on the part of the athletes. My approach was to first earn the trust of each athlete through patience and a detailed overview of what services I could offer. One of the telltale signs that I was making progress happened when both clients started bringing me a cup of coffee at the start of our meetings. Then, my objective was to encourage the athletes to learn about what makes them tick, and also, what gets in the way of great performance. Self-exploration is always a motivator, and as you will see later on in this book, athlete understanding is necessary when the objective is excellence in the ring.

Every athlete is different in terms of what makes him/her tick. In a sense, I explain to athletes at the beginning of our consulting relationship that they are "boutique operations" in the business sense of the word. What might make Athlete A perform can possibly serve no value with Athlete B, and also take away from the performance of Athlete C. The objective then is not to start with a set of pre-determined skills and approach each athlete in relation to those sport psychology skills. Arguably there are skills that each athlete can learn that will benefit performance, but those will be explained later. Rather, I start with what the athlete needs, and often, develop my skills and theories with the athletes I work with. One prime example is a theoretical framework that facilitates athlete onsite adaptation. That theory was developed with the assistance of my clients, and it is now published in respected sport psychology journals, worldwide. Not only am I a facilitator of athlete education, I am also often a student who learns from each athlete, based upon what he/she needs. From what we learn together, the athlete and I strike a solid relationship with the client's excellence and development as the target.

As I have already explained, I am not a practitioner who works by the book – at least not in terms of content. In another life, I am a Sport Psychology Professor and Canada Research Chair who specializes in multicultural approaches to sport motivation. The designation of "Canada Research Chair" is not easily earned: only well-funded international caliber researchers achieve this designation from the federal government, in collaboration with a university or learning institute. Most of my research focus is with the highest level of athletes, be they boxers, or professional ice-hockey players pursuing careers in the National Hockey League. I seek to understand and then explain what motivates each athlete in relation to his/her background. With a carefully developed approach to practice, I am able to gain the trust of my client, and, then, help him exceed performance objectives.

SO WHAT DO I MEAN BY A MENTAL EDGE?

In the title I refer to the term "mental edge". Most performances are won and lost by inches. An inch here and an inch there, amounts to a considerable distance when the preparation of two equally talented athletes are compared. I am an avid viewer of boxing footage, especially programming taped from ESPN, Show Time, and HBO. Within these three television stations, the student of boxing is provided with ample opportunity to learn about the sweet science. Study the two opponents before they enter the ring and often, you could pretty much forecast the outcome. One boxer approaches the ring with a solid focus, steps into the ring, takes a deep breath, looks to the judges, looks to the crowd, and then focuses only on his target: the opponent. The other boxer steps into the ring, either cautiously, or carelessly. His eyes seem to roam everywhere, or he averts eye contact altogether, and next, he breathes from his upper chest, panting superficially. When the two athletes touch gloves, the first athlete holds his opponent's eye contact while the second athlete looks away, with a facial expression of submissiveness and self-questioning. From there, more often than not you can guess what happens.

The amount of conviction of the two boxers just described did not result solely from decisions, leading to behaviors in the ring. The two athletes started their pathway to advancement or regression long before the sound of the bell. The result of the bout can likely be traced back to good and bad decisions taken much earlier on, perhaps even before these two athletes were scheduled to match skills. Perhaps the differences resulted from adequate versus inadequate debriefing of the previous performance, contributing to differences in understanding of what works and what does not for the athlete and those who work with him. With limited understanding for example, the athlete then could have approached his next bout with weak or unsubstantiated confidence, meaning hollow, thinly founded belief. Another possibility is that the athlete did or did not correctly learn about his opponent early enough to really become comfortable and fully familiar with the information before he needed to use it. Another option again could have traced to a correct or incorrect warm-up, with better or worse control of the dressing room before the athlete ever stepped into the ring.

The three examples I have just provided are only a few possibilities that sometimes explain why some athletes succeed where other stall in their progression. Every decision that the athlete and those who work with him/her make can be equated with an inch of distance that takes the athlete closer or further away from the end outcome of excellence. When the athlete, and his working team then come together post-bout and identify and tally the inches gained and lost leading up to and during the performance, the distance covered in terms of performance is immense. An so, every performance is won and lost by inches, inches here and inches there, all helping to explain the overall performance outcome.

I have made a point of studying professional boxers through a combination of first-hand exposure as a member of a professional boxing working team that travels the world. Adding to my experiences, I make a point of learning from the sound and weak decisions of other boxers by following only the best pugilists featured on television. Finally, I follow-up on my suspicions by engaging in scientific research with my graduate, doctoral, and post-doctoral students, and then I seek feedback on my ideas through presentations at global sport science conferences and also by sharing my views with my working team (see the dedication at the beginning of this book). The people I work with share the very same philosophy and together, we make a formidable team. Our approach to performance is the holistic marriage of boxing know-how, science, common sense, and extensive critical evaluation. The goal is to find inches that others do not even look for.

WHAT FOLLOWS

Boxing is more than a matter of guess work and it needs to be recognized that even though some might disagree, there are things to be learned through a systematic and comprehensive approach to performance. A good friend and working teammate, Russ Anber, always speaks about boxing as the "sweet science" in his television series "In this Corner". Boxing is not only a science, it is an artistic endeavor, as well. However, it is in part a science, and the science that we will cover in this book (I promise) will be also somewhat artistic, and highly intuitive. On the other hand, substantive confidence is built from know-how, and such knowledge must integrate facts and also, fact-finding.

The structure of this book will be simple and chronological. Section One reflects comprises several chapters devoted to your daily training as a boxer. Concepts such as goals, focus, a positive - constructive approach, focused training and team harmony will be discussed in detail as part of this first basic part of The Mental Edge. As you will see, Section One includes the foundational pieces / positive habits as you get closer to a bout. In Section Two we will look more closely at the aspects required for detailed and systematic bout preparation. As I mentioned earlier, some detailed thought is required in advance of performance, and the aspects described in Section Two are delivered in a manner much like a student's exam preparation. Longer-term preparation far exceeds the strategy of cramming. As parts of Section Two you will find pieces relating to personal adaptation, how to study your opponent, and how to structure the time leading up to the fight. Within Section Three, we shift to implementation and reflection. Implementation includes the strategies you can employ immediately before and during the bout. The reflection piece addresses post-bout debriefing, which then becomes the first step toward the next bout.

HOW TO USE THIS BOOK

In total, I will share some of the pieces to my approach gained working with high performance boxers engaged in an ongoing search for excellence. Of note, I have now worked with world champions and linear titlists for more than ten years. All of the clients I have worked with understood as you must understand, that the pieces of a mental edge approach might take a little time to put in place. I recall one boxer who would cut corners on the running track while engaged in his morning workouts alongside his teammates. The very same boxer also generally cut corners in his overall preparation. In relation to his mental game, the boxer seemed to re-learn from the very same mistakes many times. If this book were to be summed up in one larger mission it would be the following:

Learn lessons daily, integrate what you learn, and develop self-awareness that far exceeds that of your opponent. With your knowledge, preparation, and talent, you will become more than the sum of your parts.

Dr. Robert Schinke, Professor and Canada Research Chair in Multicultural Sport and
Physical Activity
Consultant to High Performance Boxers

SECTION ONE: DAILY STRATEGIES

Chapter 2

QUESTIONS ASKED BY BOXERS AND THEIR COACHES

Each time I meet with a new client, he has many questions to bring to the table. Asking questions is an important and necessary part of your progression as an athlete. In this chapter you will likely find a question or two that are familiar. You might also have other questions that we won't cover off here, which is perfectly fine. Remember, there is no such thing as a stupid question. Every question is a sign of intelligence and curiosity on your part. When you ask questions, you gain answers, and on a much deeper level, you gain the sort of understanding that is needed for consistent excellence. So, bottom line, ask away, and in so doing, put lingering questions to bed.

Before we get to a few general questions directly below, I have to confide in you the reason why I have added this chapter to the overall book's structure. In 2006, I published my first two scientific publications about the subject of "athlete adaptation". You will find an entire chapter (Chapter 9) devoted to the topic of adaptation. Pertinent to the present chapter, some athletes learn to adapt to extreme challenges, act, and sometimes also respond effectively, where others lower their skill level, to the point where they look much better during training, than they do in the moment of competition. After five years of my research devoted to scientific studies on why some athletes rise to the challenge of performance where others shrink from it, I have learned that athletes don't just respond to challenge in better or worse ways by chance. Instead, they adapt in sport, much like we all must adapt to any changing circumstance in life, hopefully by making sound choices, built from a constructive – solution oriented approach.

Sound choices don't just happen, at least not on a consistent basis. Sound decisions, which are the foundation for the positive actions that follow, are built from a solid and thorough understanding of relevant information. Understanding comes from asking questions, lots and lots of questions. If our questions are answered, either by personal experience, another person, or through a formal investigation that we embark on through reading and watching footage of ourselves and other boxers, only then can we say why we have wisely chosen one decision over a wide number of options. You make many decisions every day, some of those decisions are mundane and less important; others are more significant. The key is to that you become informed regarding decisions that are important to you, and from understanding, embark down the correct pathway to success.

The world champions I work with are always asked why they have chosen one decision over another. When the client effectively answers the "why", he then knows what basis there is for his certainty leading up to the next performance. From knowing the why behind his decisions, that athlete gains in knowledge and a substantive confidence built from facts and not fiction or guesswork. In relation to this chapter, the questions we are considering belong in the category of self-understanding. Self-understanding is the starting point to a more comprehensive approach to understanding that we will speak about in Chapter Ten. For now, let's go through a few of the questions that have been asked to me consistently by my best clients, over time. Remember, you might have other questions than the ones I consider below. The important point is to pursue answers to your questions proactively so that you know what you need to know before it really matters, and not only after the fact. Asking questions after a setback is a strategy that many athletes do. In this case, try to be one of the few, and not one of the many.

Why Do I Need a Mental Game Plan – I've Done Fine to this Point?

Believe it or not, you likely have many of the pieces of a mental game plan in place, already. If you think you don't have a mental game plan, consider my argument and line of thinking: I will bet you have certain meals that sit well with you before you train or compete. You likely also know the quantity of rest required for a very good day of training, and also, in advance of a performance. When you enter the gym, likely you engage in a warm-up process that includes a narrowing of focus, including a physically progressive warm-up, a peak period, and then, a cool down. Some of what you do daily, might also transfer onto the day of competition. There are likely strategies from your coaches that work better for you in the corner before and during sparring, and likely coaches' strategies that also work on fight night. You get the picture, there are things that you do daily as a boxer that are in fact part of your mental game plan. When a warm-up structure is changed, I will bet that it irritates you and causes you to respond with some strategies as you attempt your return to a routine, even if it is in a modified format. The format you engage reflects that fact that you indeed have a mental game plan.

When I begin working with even an experienced professional boxer, there is extensive understanding on the part of that boxer already in terms of what works for him. What I do is sell the client on the idea that we need to go looking at least a little bit deeper into his planning decisions – meaning things that together we identify to further refine his plan. Some athletes choose not to engage in self-discovery and opt to stay with what works for them, without looking inward, systematically. More often than not, these are the athletes that either never make it to the pinnacle of their capabilities, or if they become accomplished, their reign at the top is shortened by poor decisions and a lack of understanding of what constitutes a good decision versus a bad one. So, for such athletes, bad decisions come as often as good decisions, and sometimes it becomes unpredictable to know whether a decision will move the athlete forward or backward.

I recall some years ago I was pulled into two consecutives team meetings, the first with a world champion boxer and his staff. The boxer was scheduled to defend his world title four months later against a very experienced and dangerous opponent. The athlete's promoter knew the athlete was not prepared for the task of what was to come and so, the promoter tried to build a more comprehensive working team around the athlete. When the athlete was offered sport science services, including my own and a few additional resources, his response was that he was accomplished and successful without the proposed resources – why change now? When the discussion continued, it became very clear that the athlete lacked the necessary knowledge and critical pieces to effectively defend his title. Even when the boxer was told that without extensive help, he would jeopardize his status, there was an unwillingness to engage in self-discovery, and as part of that process, the development of a much stronger mental game. When the weigh-in followed a few months later, the day before the fight, the champion averted the gaze of his opponent. In contrast, the opponent looked highly focused, and as predicted, ready to move forward - onward to champion's status. The next day, one champion was dethroned, and a new one, crowned.

During the very same meeting day when one champion, discussed directly above, decided to step away from self-discovery, a much younger boxer met with the very same team. The younger boxer was no stranger to a sport science approach, given that he resourced similar services during a reasonably successful amateur career. That day became a pivotal moment and a tipping point to the positive for the young prospect. He stepped forward and started putting in place sport science resources that he was comfortable with, me included. Within one year he fought for a world title in a fight that was voted the most exciting fight of the year. Even though the athlete lost the bout, he grew in confidence, rebounded very quickly, and then became a world champion, and afterward, a linear king of his division and a *Ring Champion*. There are very few Ring Champions crowned, as these athletes are identified across the alphabet titles as "the boxer" – lion in his weight division.

Open-mindedness is critical, with every developing boxer requiring a willingness to learn and progress, not only in terms of the technical parts of the sport, but also in the areas of tactics and psychology. Tactics and psychology go hand in hand, and together, they arm the athlete with a mental edge that more often than not, will allow him to overcome great obstacles, including a more experienced, odds-on favorite.

So, why do you need a mental game plan? The answer is that you already have the makings of one, built from intuitive knowledge and the guidance of your coaches and teammates. The objective is to push that plan further, make it deeper, and most important, built from a sound systematic approach that addresses the question "why". From a solid scientific approach to boxing, you will have more than just hollow confidence that wavers from one performance to the next. If you haven't already, you will feel, time and again, a solid confidence that stands up to the most challenging pressures you will encounter in your journey to the top. Finally, remember that the term game plan includes the word "plan". Planning is something we work on and revise with the completion of every performance, until it becomes a finely tuned structure, reflecting you as an individual – boutique operation. Remember that what works for one boxer might now work for another, and plans also do evolve over time. Great boxers need to be progressive in their thinking.

WHAT READING MATERIALS AND VISUAL RESOURCES ARE AVAILABLE TO ME?

Many of my athletes engage in extensive reading as part of a more general search for knowledge. I suppose that is the reason why I have written this book! Knowledge can be gained from several different learning opportunities that you might or might not have already considered. In terms of reading, there is much to learn from general motivational books. In fact, of the many national team and professional athletes I have worked with over nearly twenty years in the business, boxers are the most well read athletes, on average. I have seen clients read the likes of Anthony Robbins, Stephen Covey, and Martin Seligman, and I agree with the general approach of reading and evaluating at least some of the motivational strategies offered up. There is much to learn from motivational authors.

In addition, there is a wealth of published sport psychology material accessible to you, well beyond the present book. Sport psychology is a growing profession, now with regulatory guidelines, certification programs, and formal degrees, through to the doctoral level. With the development of the field, new and innovative authors are being published all the time, each with a slightly different take on how to pursue athletic excellence. Publishers such as Nova Science (the publishing house for this book) is among the companies that now feature advanced, though accessible readings for sport scientists, but also for you, the athlete, with feet based solidly in the applied domain of sport. Search the net and consider the vast number of potential resources you can consider as reading material.

There are also professional sport science publications, developed for coaches and athletes. These sorts of writings are usually crafted into every day language. Academics tend to use words that outside of their field might mean nothing at all – that sort of language is simply jargon. I always send my most engaged athletes and coaches, professional publications to fuel their knowledge. More times than not, they in turn come back to me with questions. Their questions in turn, build shared understanding, and a much deeper exchange among the working team. The athlete is always at the center of any working team, so my expectation is for the athlete to read and learn at least as much as the other members, though hopefully, more.

Another source of written material that I gravitate toward is boxing magazines written for general enthusiasts, such as *Ring Magazine* – one of my favorites. Within such materials are different sorts of resources that can contribute to your growing knowledge as an athlete and student of the sport. One prime example is the monthly contribution from Bernard Hopkins. Within his contribution, BHop shares ideas relating to ring generalship, which in turn can be discussed with your coach and perhaps, integrated as part of sparring and eventual performance. In addition, there are athlete features, including stories about emerging star Odlanier Solis, a former Cuban Olympic Champion, who is now well on his way to a successful professional career as a heavyweight. From the athlete features, you could begin to look at the sort of team such athletes surround themselves with, as well as their general philosophical approach to the game. Of note, sometimes athlete features can also indicate when an athlete lacks focus. Finally, in such magazines there are reviews of higher profile performances. Small bites of information can be gained if you read about series of fights within and across installments, providing hints regarding why boxers move forward and step back in their careers based upon their tactics in the ring.

Beyond what you can gain from reading, as I indicated in the last chapter, much can be learned from viewing televised bouts, especially those that feature the boxer in the lead up to the fight, and then, the actual fight, and the post-bout interviews with knowledgeable commentators such as Larry Merchant and Max Kellerman, on HBO, or Steve Farhoud and Antonio Tarver, on ShowTime. The lead-up to the fight provides useful information about how the athlete orients himself before the fight and as part of that orientation, how he evaluates his opponent. One can easily see even when an athlete does not disclose the details, when he is knowledgeable about his opponent, and when he has chosen the path to poor mental preparation and a general approach to the fight. Then, by watching the fight, one can easily learn the do's and don'ts hidden in final warm-ups, the walk to the ring, entry into the ring, and the festivities that come before the actual performance, each a place where sometimes, outcomes are won or lost. Within the fight, one can learn how tactics are employed and sometimes also surrendered. Usually the move forward in plan implementation or backwards and away from one's plan is usually also associated with facial expressions that serve as dead giveaways. Between rounds it is worthwhile looking at communication and protocol within the athlete's corner. Sometimes corners are perfectly composed, harmonious, and clear in their strategies and words. Other times, chaos in the corner plays havoc on the athlete's performance within the following round, and also potentially over the course of an entire fight. And after the bout, the words shared by each athlete are perhaps his most honest and accurate regarding his performance, and also, even his next performance.

All told, there are pockets of useful knowledge available to you. Some of those resources are actually at your very fingertips, should you choose to take the time and study. My thought is that every emerging athlete could deepen his knowledge and substance as a boxer, by becoming a student of the sport. People like Bernard Hopkins, the Klitchko's, and also some of the new faces in the sport today such as Andre Ward and Jean Pascal have taken such a progressive approach to boxing. Though I obviously argue in favor of studying, given that I am an academic researcher and professor, be assured that by taking a student's approach to boxing you will gift yourself with knowledge, and from that knowledge, power. That power will in turn surface in the ring when you need it most. As a result, you will become one of those athletes who improve in quality under challenge, and not an athlete who lowers his standards.

How Can I Find a Mental Training Consultant or Sport Psychologist Who Suits My Needs?

There is no easy answer to finding the right consultant. As I indicated earlier, sport psychology is a profession that is growing in sheer numbers of applied consultants. There are many programs in universities around the world that now offer up sport psychology programs. I have collaborated with sport psychologists in Japan, China, Russia, Sweden, Germany, Ghana, Nigeria, England, Australia, Singapore, the United States, New Zealand, Columbia, and Canada. The countries above are only a few examples of locations you might find solid practicing consultants. Surf the net and you will find the vast numbers of people at your fingertips.

Now that you appreciate the large number of consultants available to athletes, you might consider that some of the people offer services that are educational in nature, acquired through a Physical Education or Education degree. I am one such person. Mental training consultants, as we are termed, have studied sport psychology literature, but their training and degrees orient them toward performance enhancement, and not clinical subjects, such as eating disorders, espisodic depression, nor any type of clinical diagnosis. There are also clinical psychologists with formal Psychology degrees, at least of a graduate level. These people are more apt to work with athletes who struggle with more general life challenges outside of performance, but they similar to the mental training consultant, might also work in performance enhancement. So how do you choose between the two types of resources? In some cases it is a matter of preference. In other cases, clinical psychologists are the correct resource on matters that are "clinical".

There is also the matter of consultant certification. Associations including the Association of Applied Sport Psychology and the Canadian Sport Psychology Association evaluate their members in terms of core competencies, such as the number of formal sport psychology, clinical psychology, social psychology, sport science, and ethics courses taken. In addition, more often than not, vetting also includes amassed supervisory hours under an experienced practitioner, where the young consultant can practice skills and refine those skills under supervision during a set amount of hours of observation.

You might also wish to consider the applied background of the consultant. Some work exclusively with team athletes, others with athletes from individual sport, some specialize in youth sport, other in elite amateur sport, and still others, almost exclusively with professional sport. Within specializations, you can also investigate the sorts of topics and skills the consultant specializes in, such as resilience training, mental training, self-confidence, or whether they take a broad-based approach, where they employ a wide number of skills as part of their service. In learning about the consultant's preferences, explore the web and see whether the consultant has published in a specific area. Though many fantastic consultants do not publish, for those who do, their publishing area might provide some indication of what their best-developed skills are. Mine happen to be in performance preparation, opponent profiling, athlete adaptation, and culturally relevant strategies. Each consultant likely has specialties where they are well read. Also, remember, no consultant is an expert in everything!

Finally, there is the gut feeling you have when you first meet a motivational consultant. The feeling you should have is a sense of being comfortable when sharing your background, and the areas you wish to learn about and develop as an athlete. The person on the other end of the exchange, meaning the consultant, should be a very good listener, have the ability to ask important questions that clarify your thinking, and also leave you with some takeaway reflections that are facilitative of your progression. In addition, the consultant needs to be accessible to you when you need him/her, and there needs to be a willingness on the part of the consultant to work with you according to your timeframe. If you need him/her quickly, then he must be quickly accessible.

As you can see, there are a few considerations that factor into who you choose as a sport psychology professional. Sometimes athletes choose their provider without much thought and the choice works out wonderfully. The considerations I have just provided are simply that – considerations for you to consider.

SHOULD I TRACK MY PROGRESS?

Before I began working in professional boxing, I worked first with the Canadian National Boxing Team. In the years of 1998 and 1999 the team had record level results at the Commonwealth Games and Pan-American Games. The results at the Commonwealth Games included 10 medals earned by 12 athletes, with five of those athletes winning gold medals. One year later, before the 1999 Pan-American Games, I was told with some skepticism by a member of the team's staff not to have too high an expectation in terms of medals; the previous best performance was three medals at a single Pan-Am. On both counts, the team results were not achieved by accident. During pre-tournament training camps, I worked very closely with each athlete and the coach assigned to work his corner. The topic of discussion was competition planning. Together we considered what needed to happen the night before the bout, throughout the day, what needed to be packed, when to arrive onsite at the tournament venue, what the warm-up structure would be, how to walk to the ring, how to structure each round, and what worked best in terms of corner work.

The athletes already knew some of what worked best for them, but in every case new things were identified by asking the question: "what would bring out the best in me as a performer?" After each day of athlete-coach discussions, coaches' meetings were held to discuss the profiles of individual athletes as boutique operations. As we discussed the cases, the coach assigned to the given athlete took notes and we condensed down the points onto index cards, with strategies customized for the athlete. Some might propose that by asking the athletes what they needed, even deeper trust was earned with the coaching staff, leading to more assertive decisions in the ring. You might correctly also point out that the exercise of coordinating communication between the athlete and the coach enhanced the overall performance of the athlete, ending in tangible medals. Both points are correct. In addition though, what we achieved through the sit-down exercise was the formalizing of a bout strategy, confirmed by the athlete. As each athlete formalized his ideas, he began a few weeks before the tournament, down a path of knowing how his plan would unfold.

After the 1998 record tally of medals, the team more than doubled its medals the following year at the 1999 Pan-American Games and finished with seven from 12 athletes, with five athletes boxing in the finals. In advance of that tournament, we built on the athletes' performance preferences from the previous year and considered how to refine each profile. Then again, with the athletes say so, the coaching staff worked together to summarize athletes' preferences in a revised format. With the know how of how to bring out the best in themselves and their coaches, the athletes were in fact engaged in evaluating their performance from one year to the next.

You need to learn skills and develop a strategy to log those insights so that you keep what you've learned for the long-term. I have seen more athletes than not have a tremendous day of training or a fantastic performance, and immediately after admit that they did something different that seemed to make the difference in their performance. The athlete then soon forgets his recent insight, only to re-learn it again six months later. When I hear stories of "re-learning" I always think about the gross inefficiency associated with having to re-learn the same lesson twice, and in some cases many times over the span of an entire boxing career.

So how can you track your progress? Write down your insights in a performance log and know that you now have them for safekeeping and re-use. When we move to Chapter 13 there will be an extensive explanation of how you might track down the details of best practice. For now though, if you learn something new today or tomorrow, write it down in a notebook that eventually will become your performance log and the psychological key to your mental performance package.

Remember that earlier I explained the importance of understanding yourself. Substantive confidence is built from know how - not guess work. As an aspiring boxer you need to be in part a sport scientists on the subject of "you". You need to understand what brings out the best in you and also, what takes away from your mental edge. With knowledge built from an ongoing refined fact finding mission, you will know what steps needs to be taken, why they need to be taken, and how to go about taking those steps. Performance is built from facts, not fiction, and definitely not from speculation. Commit to self-awareness and at the same time you will be well on your way to sustained excellence.

FINAL REFLECTIONS

Questions are an opportunity for learning. There are critical points in a bout when it is not the time to ask questions, but rather to go with what you know and what your coaches confirm. During training though, there is lots of time and reason to ask questions and learn about you as a student of boxing. You can agree that answers come from questions, usually as a chronology, with questions coming first.

From questions, sometimes, initial answers are not satisfying. You might have a gut instinct that there is more to the answer than you and those around you can provide. When parts of a question are unanswered, or not answered to your satisfaction, you have the power to dig deeper. There are many creditable websites, discussion forums, video footage, professional magazines, and sport science materials for you to draw on. Take the necessary time to answer the questions that arise through daily evolution.

Today's question should lead to tomorrow's answer, and likely also, new questions, leading to continuous s-evolution. When you open yourself up to learning, and allow your curiosity to flourish, you also deepen your knowledge as a student of the sport. From depth of knowledge comes a level of confidence that stands up to most any challenge that you will encounter in and out of the ring. By moving forward in discovery, you will also be confirming another very good instinct, and that is learning proactively and not from unnecessary lessons and setbacks. You only have a finite time to learn as an athlete – don't squander it away through inefficiency. You have the power to learn, and from learning comes sound decisions, good results, and ongoing progression – right to the top.

Chapter 3

UNPACKING THE PIECES OF A MENTAL GAME PLAN

There are many pieces to a boxer's mental game plan. When I watch boxers fight on ESPN and Show Time, there is mention from commentators, including Teddy Atlas and Antonio Tarver about mental toughness, mental fortitude, and desire. These words resurface through commentary time and again, in advance of a high profile fights. After the bout, again, there is discussion about one athlete having imposed his will and tactics over the other. Boxing is one of those sports where there is lots of lip service paid to the mental part of the game. Experts realize that when an athlete is mentally prepared for the challenge of his opponent and the surrounding challenges related to the bout, he will perform well. The mental game, then, seems to be a significant part of the boxer's performance outcome.

One can easily talk about the mental game, but really what are they talking about? Does mental toughness in the ring just materialize out of thin air? Is it solely a matter of correct technical training, paired with good tactical decisions? Or, can we take apart the psychological pieces needed as part of an athlete's mental package, learn them, assemble them, and re-package that athlete into a product better than he otherwise could be? You will find in this chapter that the mental game is a matter of pieces, assembled into one larger mental game plan, then in turn can provide you with the competitive edge you are looking for.

So what are the pieces of a mental game plan? Well, you could definitely benefit from the following:

- Positive clear – specific goals
- A solid focus while training
- Strong communication skills
- A positive – constructive mindset
- Organizational skills
- Adaptation skills
- Pre-bout preparation
- Knowledge of the opponent
- A plan for the day of the bout
- The correct warm-up structure
- Tactics for the walk to and entry into the ring

- In the moment focus
- A debriefing strategy

What follows is a brief operational description of each point above so that you develop a working knowledge of the terminology that will be discussed as we move deeper into the book. Though some of the pieces before us will be more important to you at a given moment in your development, all of these pieces, together, will provide you with a comprehensive package and the sort of mental package that will lead to the mental edge you are looking for.

POSITIVE – CLEAR - SPECIFIC GOALS

We all have the capacity to set goals. Sadly, for many boxers, based on how they set their goals, those goals don't work as well as they should. I have asked many a boxer what his/her objective is – only to be answered with "to become the best boxer I can be". I agree that becoming a better boxer is suggestive of a positive approach to the sport. However, when you set your goals you need to be far more specific in terms of what being an improved boxer means to you. Goals need to be more than generally positive - they must also be very precise. You might choose to be a strong inside fighter, a boxer with smooth, well-timed lateral movement, a quick starter, a patient counter puncher, or a relentless aggressor who wears down opponents. All of these attributes are skills regarded by at least some boxers as worthy of their focus. You need to identify the targeted skills you are seeking to develop. Move beyond general terms such as great, best, positive, and tough. Instead, go the next step and ask yourself what you really want within a given term and chisel down the term to a discussion point – something you can sink your teeth into and work toward.

Goals then are not generalities for people to throw around during conversation. They are directional markers that are carefully chosen in consultation with your coach to move you from one level of development, onward to the next level of development. Correctly crafted, goals are meant to serve as guideposts, but also, consistent reminders of where you are going, in relation to where you presently are. Correctly developed goals will help you become much more efficient in your evolution as a boxer. From good goals, comes good – correctly directed focus. On the other hand, if you develop general goals, goals that are too easy, or irrelevant goals, your progression will be delayed through incorrect navigation, toward a direction that may not serve as performance enhancing. In Chapter 4 (the next chapter) we will look in-depth at how to set effective goals, as part of a positive vision.

FOCUS WHILE TRAINING

During countless presentations with aspiring boxers, I have always asked those sitting in the room to raise their hands if they think they have a strong focus when training. More often than not, most, if not all athletes raise their hands. Then I go a little deeper and ask who among the group set a goal for today's training, before walking into the gym? In response only the occasional boxer ever raises his/her hand. People think they have a good focus until someone really challenges them to think and take stock of why they believe they have a good focus. Confidence in your skills, as I have already shared with you, cannot be hollow. Confidence needs to be solid, built from facts. When I ask my clients questions relating to any part of their mental game plan, including their focus, they should be able to answer those questions with clear and precise answers, and also, facts that support their position. The capacity to respond to the positive regarding your use of mental skills affirms who you are, and why you will succeed in your goals, through extensive focus.

Focus is not just a general term for you to throw around, claiming that you have a "good focus". Instead, focus is something you need to commit to as part of each day's training. Focusing on the day's training is meant to happen before you step into the gym, as you step into the gym, while you get changed, and as you stretch, skip rope, and then start shadow boxing. Focus for most athletes is something they warm into after some extensive pad- work, bag work, or sparring. I propose that focus is not a sometimes skill, but rather, an all the time skills. If you develop good focus in relation to training, what do you think will be your habit within a bout? Focus is developed much like a muscle – through practice. The opposite holds true, also. If you have inconsistent focus in training, what sort of focus do you think will surface under pressure during a performance? You guessed – a wavering focus. In Chapter 5 we will look much more closely at the importance of good focus, and afterward, how you can develop a good focus that will be there when you need it most.

STRONG COMMUNICATION SKILLS

Most everyone thinks he has strong communication skills. To become a progressive boxer, you need to really work away on communication skills, all of the time. When athletes communicate well, they are free to focus on performance, and not a pile of distractions that have been built up through words that are unsaid, and problems that are unresolved. Your focus must be directed on a single target / objective, for you really to perform to your potential. A member of the working team I am part of is well known within the amateur boxing community: Dr. Pedro Diaz. Pedro is a former national team coach for the Cuban National Boxing Team, in the times when Cuba dominated Olympics and World Championships. Pedro speaks every day about the importance of positive energy. I have learned that positive energy in part originates from positive and open communication. Positive energy is passed on from one person to another, in some cases through correct communication.

Over the course of the last decade, I have worked with several successful professional world champion boxers. Each time one of my clients is crowned as world champion, I look back over his training camp and reflect at how his/her team pulled together. Each member of the team understood his role, and the contribution of that role as part of the larger team's objective. In my earlier days, I also worked as part of a team, where the team fell apart due to either laziness or a lack of communication amongst the athlete and his working team. When things are left unsaid between an athlete and his support system, or between the support system and the athlete, or across a support system, performance always declines. The athlete's decline might not be immediate, but it is inevitable. Even when things are going well within my working teams, we have daily meetings, many heated discussions, and always, a search for even better solutions. The athlete is always the beneficiary of good communication. Sadly, when communication falls apart, even the best athlete becomes a sitting duck, and inevitably, the person who loses most. In Chapter 6 we will delve into the topic of communication, and how to facilitate better communication, that in turn contributes to boxing excellence.

A POSITIVE - CONSTRUCTIVE MINDSET

Your psychological foundation must also include a positive – constructive way of thinking. During my doctorate, I spent four years interviewing successful and less successful Canadian Olympians in terms of their perspective. Some of the athletes were very constructive, solution-oriented thinkers, where others were negative and problem-oriented. When the two groups were compared as part of the research project, those who were positive -minded progressed much faster as Olympians, and often achieved Olympic medals within their first four year cycle on their national team, meaning their first attempt at an Olympics. The problem-oriented athletes were much slower to progress, and often, those athletes became weighed down in poor communication, conflict, apathy, and lower quality performances. After I completed my doctorate, I was able to spend one year in post-doctoral research developing training modules for Olympic level athletes and their coaches. The objective through the training was to teach the coaches, who then would teach their athletes, solution oriented thinking as part of each day's training. The modules are now being delivered each year through Canada's National Coaching Institute to its high-performance full-time coaches.

Constructive thinking is a habit, and there are ways to develop solution-oriented thought. The skills required are built from how you choose to describe yourself and those around you, through language. The words we choose are more meaningful and critical than you might initially think. With Chapter 7 we will look in-depth at how you, with the help of those who support you, can develop a positive way of thinking and speaking that in turn, contributes to positive focus and positive performance. When we tackle Chapter 7 you will likely be surprised about how importance of the power of positive and negative thinking really is. One thing is for certain: the skill set of constructive thinking will take you more than one step closer to your potential.

ORGANIZATIONAL SKILLS

Athletes on the pathway to success must also be extremely well organized. Great organization is a matter of knowing how to structure a year's boxing development in a way that makes more than just intuitive sense. Within the sport psychology and cognitive psychology research, over the course of more than 30 years, there has been a vibrant discussion regarding how expert performers across disciplines including sport, develop their talents into concrete high-level success through well-structured training sessions. Though talent is a very important characteristic for most every aspiring athlete, in and of itself, talent is over-rated. Equally important to the athlete is his willingness to make correct decisions, based on a strong organizational approach to training and also, competition.

From the extensive research out there in the public domain, it is well known that most every top-class athlete devotes himself to more than 10,000 hours of well-organized training in order to reach the level of performance necessary to withstand the challenges posed within sport. Relating to boxing, you need to invest approximately 10 years of carefully crafted training and competition in order for you as a talented athlete, to reach your elite level potential. There are of course boxers who have a meteoric rise to the top, based on a high knock out percentage. Even for such athletes, when they eventually meet an athlete of the very same experience, with better-organized training under their belts, all of a sudden the athletes with the high KO percentages fade. Take for example Edison Miranda, who eventually met his match with Kelly Pavlik – a better skilled boxer with more amateur background. The bottom line is that you need to be extremely well organized within each hour's training in order to build the skills that not only will bring you to a high level of boxing, but also develop you beyond the average elite boxer, and into a long-standing performer in the ring. On the other hand, every hour of training or performance lost through weak focus, should be viewed as an opportunity lost. Good organization skills, like good concentration skills, good communication skills, and a positive approach, needs to be considered as a habit. The habit of being organized each day will be an essential part of who you will become, and if you think you are already highly organized, after you read Chapter 8, expect to bring your organizational skills to a higher level, again.

ADAPTATION SKILLS

Throughout the first two chapters of this book, I have touched a few times on the topic of adaptation and why it is important to your overall performance. Adaptation is a response that each one of us engages in when we confront a challenge that is more than what we are accustomed to. When you encounter a significant challenge such as a more experienced and higher profile opponent, or a tournament that is higher profile and more pressure filled than anything you have experienced in the past, the ultimate objective is for you to respond positively, and showcase your skills. As I indicated already, some athletes respond to challenge by increasing their efforts and excelling in dire circumstances, where others decrease their efforts and relinquish control over their competition plan, to the benefit of the opponent.

As you can see only some athletes adapt where others retreat in response to significant career challenges. If you are following the Super Six Tournament on ShowTime, you can see that few are the competitors that perform when asked to box out of town. Is there really a hometown advantage in boxing, and if so, it is always telling of a win and a loss? I would think that when athletes feel they have a hometown advantage, they increase their efforts and perform to potential. Inversely, it seems to make sense that when a boxer is fighting out of town and sees the adversities that surround travel as overwhelming, he will decrease his efforts and so, become more often than not, the bout's loser. The objective I am proposing to you is that wherever you travel, you must adapt. After all, not every Olympic Gold Medal boxer won his medal in his home country. Adaptive thinking takes each of us a long way toward excellence. Within Chapter 9 you will find a detailed series of strategies to help you with adaptation. You need to be one of those athletes who excel under challenge, and if you are wondering how to do so, Chapter 9 might contain the answers you are looking for.

PRE-BOUT PREPARATION

Much of my work is devoted to pre-bout preparation when I work with high profile professional athletes. The objective is always to build a performance plan that at very least maintains the athlete's performance level from training into competition. Many times, athletes look much better in training than they do in competition. Such athletes are referred to as backyard performers. Others actually compete at a much higher level on fight night than they do in training. Some wonder what the differences are between these two types of athletes. Though parts of the answer to increased and decreased levels of performance can be answered in other chapters, one piece of the puzzle can be found in pre-bout preparation. I will bet that you have experienced high school exams at some point in your life. As part of every student's experiences as a scholar he/she has studied several days in advance of an exam, and also tried in at least a few instances to study entirely the morning of the exam. Which of the two studying strategies just provided do you think leads to a better result? Obviously longer-term preparation is the better studying practice because time allows you the opportunity to really understand when you need to deliver during the exam, and moreover, extended studying allows you to interpret the knowledge before you and integrate it in unique ways. Interpretation and reflection take time and they cannot be rushed.

Pre-bout preparation takes more than just time, however. You must also take into account not only what you have studied generally in the earlier chapters. In addition you need to now consider how you would like to press into action what you know about yourself on fight night. Afterward you need to work through your strategies during focused discussions and then during training. For example, in the weeks leading up to the fight, all of the boxers that my working team engages with work on correctly walking to and stepping into the ring in a way that will match with fight night. By the time the boxer actually steps into the ring on fight night, the process of entering the ring is well-established, and it is also correctly followed through. In Chapter 10 we will look much more closely at the pre-performance strategies that will transition you from a general training mentality to a performance mentality as fight night draws nearer.

KNOWLEDGE OF THE OPPONENT

Through Chapter 10, the focus is placed squarely on self-awareness, meaning that most of the work is devoted to you learning about yourself, and what brings out the best in "you". There is also some importance to learning what you can about the opponent you will encounter in either a day's sparring, or within an exhibition bout, or important tournament. As I indicated to you already, before I began working with professional boxers, I spent several years traveling to national and international tournaments with elite amateur boxers. From those experiences, I was always amazed that in most countries, athletes did not take the time to really consider their opponents' characteristics before stepping in the ring. Typical practices with elite amateur sport were for boxers to slowly warm into their strategy through a prolonged / extended feeling out process within the fight. Some athletes would even refer to themselves as "slow starters". Others would say that they liked an extensive feeling out process before they really went to work in the ring and imposed themselves on the other athlete, assuming they had the confidence to impose their skills, at all. I wondered for a few years why my clients and many of the boxers from other countries took so long to warm into performance. I knew that the amount of time adjusting to the opponent determined which athletes were efficient versus inefficient. So, what factors differentiated the more from the less efficient boxers in the ring?

One of the critical pieces to the sport psychology puzzle is the capacity to adjust very quickly to the opponent in front of you, or better yet, have that opponent engage in a search for adjustment strategies in relation to your bout strategy as you take the first few rounds. Boxing performance is in a very basic way similar to any other performance – the performer needs to be extremely well prepared for what he/she is about to experience, before the performance is encountered. Sun Tsu's Art of War has been quoted religiously in relation all kinds of life battles. The quotation goes something like this: "The war should be won before it is ever fought". In relation to you as a boxer, part of any bout preparation you engage in has to be in part crafted in relation to your opponent. When athletes and their coaches try to craft the basis of a strategy a few hours before the fight, they are often too late. Have you ever tried to retain information learned on the day of an exam or life test? How much of that information is really retained when you step into the pressure cooker context of performance? The answer to my questions is that more often than not, information discussed in the short-term is forgotten. The earlier in advance of the bout you begin to study the opponent – the better. Longer-term information is retained at a much deeper level in our memory, and the key to a complete performance in the ring is the integration of deeply planted understanding not only of yourself, but also, of the opponent. Chapter 11 will be devoted to the topic of studying the opponent. The objective is for you to learn about your opponent and from what you learn, impose your will over his.

A PLAN FOR THE DAY OF THE BOUT

Successes and setbacks are sometimes explained by the decisions that boxers make during the final few hours before a fight. The basis of good decisions is a correctly designed plan for the day of the fight. When boxers and their working team work together to design plans for the day of the fight, it is relatively easy to map out a structure that makes sense and seems easy to follow. Yet, in some cases boxers forget or let go of their fight day structures and instead, begin a day's course that takes them away from the successful performance they have been building toward. Good decisions are a matter of the correct amount of sleep at the correct time of day, well chosen meals, also at essential times of day in relation to the up coming performance, who to associate it during the day and what things a support system should and should not discuss as the day's hours are counted down, and when and how to pack for the performance, among a number of other items we will consider in Chapter 12.

Given that the day's structure is important to your performance, you need to design that structure with care, and then equally important, you need to commit to that structure. Your plan for the day of the bout will be your commitment to short-term organization, though also, your working team will require equal commitment to the day's plan. Through Chapter 12 we will look much more closely at what your day's plan can look like, built from essential pieces that together, will reinforce your confidence. More often than not, when people struggle with the upcoming stress of competition, they abandon their plan and try to supplement that plan with something new and improved. Little do they know that as they engage in a search for better strategies, much too close to the fight, they have already given up some of the personal control that they will need in the fast approaching bout. Your confidence is built from sound organization, though all the best organization in the world becomes useless if it is not executed with conviction.

THE CORRECT WARM-UP STRUCTURE

Over the years, I have helped craft the warm-up structure for many promising boxers. Sometimes my involvement in the refinement of a warm-up structure has been very involved, other times I have been asked to simply be onsite should the athlete become nervous in the final few hours before he steps into the ring. Though you might not fully believe it, many a bout has been won or lost in the final few hours in the dressing room or warm-up space as the athlete starts to warm into his performance. When I think back to my experiences in dressing rooms before world championship bouts, I recall one athlete whose management team insisted on having more than 20 people sitting in the room as a supportive strategy for the athlete. With every correct punch that the athlete landed during his pad work, the room would erupt into applause. In working with a second boxer, he was under the belief that he needed several people to warm him up before the bout. Included within the warm-up structure were a massage therapist, a physiologist, and two members of his coaching team. Each of these members physically handed the athlete as the night's warm-up structure was followed.

Believe it or not, I am an advocate of simple though carefully structured warm-up protocols. There is not ever one clearly defined protocol as every athletes, as you might recall, is a boutique operation. Some athletes need more time to warm in as compared with others. Where some athletes need intermittent pad work, others might benefit from pad work structured much like a round of boxing. As well, every athlete warms in relation to his opponent's style and anticipated tactics. In Chapter 13 we will look very closely at why the two cases just described were not really optimal warm-up structures, and why. The purpose through Chapter 13 is for you to walk away with a deep understanding of how to collaborate with your working team and craft a winning warm-up structure.

TACTICS FOR THE WALK TO AND ENTRY INTO THE RING

The tactics surrounding the final minutes before the performance need to bring you closer yet to top-level performance. Whether you are an amateur boxer fighting in the Ringside Tournament or a professional boxer readying to do battle in a high profile bout, the last few minutes of time spent during your walk to the ring and your entry into the ring can make a profound difference in terms of your thinking and doing, especially during the early minutes of the bout that follow shortly thereafter. The walk is a matter of timing, meaning it should take just enough time for you to stay loose, but not more than enough time so that you are then being rushed along by your working team. Involved in the walk, you also need to have a good swagger and an imposing posture. When people open up their postures, they are always more confident than when their shoulders are slouched. Next, when entering the ring, the focus needs to narrow from the audience, to the judges, inward until you lock eyes with the opponent.

When I observe athletes before a fight, I can usually predict how they will start their fight and whether they will impose themselves on the opponent based on the simple, yet critical walk and entrance into the ring. Actions during this short finite journey need to be definitive and affirming of who you are, and what you are capable of. Solid, open postures suggest confidence and dominance. Solid, correctly directed focus suggests energy that is being invested on the correct target. Though few athletes give much thought to their walk and entrance strategies, if you study the approach taken by Iron Mike Tyson when he was at his best, you get to the essence of what an imposing – assertive approach is meant to be. Because there is no one entire approach to these final few minutes pre-bout, during Chapter 14 we will discuss a few consistent strategies that need to be taken regardless of your individual – boutique approach to performance. In addition though, we will also search for unique aspects that you can press into action that suit you, and the objective you have for the bout.

IN THE MOMENT FOCUS

Performance in the ring is ultimately as we say, where "the tire meets the road". You can expect that a well-prepared student of the game will be the most likely to perform time and again at his/her best. What happens in the ring becomes the acid test of your training and tailored preparation. The most challenging thing to do is to box in the present, meaning with your focus located only on what you and your opponent are doing, at the very split second you are each trying to do it. Earlier, I mentioned that in the moment focus is something you need to practice each day when there is little to no pressure associated with your boxing. If you have solid concentration skills in training, you are more likely to have them during performance. However, there are a few distinct differences between training and performance. One difference is that the time you previously invested in training is often for the purpose of competition. So, there is much more emotional investment in the results associated with competition as compared to a day's training. Second, competition environments are always a little more complicated than training environments due to the variables of officiating, judging, a difference in venue, and also, what is emotionally at stake in terms of winning and losing.

One of the critical discussions I engage in with every world-class boxer is the importance of mental discipline within his bout. Part of the discussion covers off being in the present from the beginning to the end of each round. Another piece of the discussion spans the importance of staying focused on the fight as the boxer goes deeper into the bout, from one round to the next. With one client I worked with some years ago, the client was defending a high profile professional belt, earned a few fights earlier. The opponent was relentless, though not in the same talent pool as my client. Part way through the fight, my client started taunting his opponent, and having won all the rounds leading to the final round, he paid for his loss of focus by getting caught with a punch, penetrated due to a sloppy defense. My client barely escaped with his title. In the moment focus is something that every boxer must learn and then remember time and again through to the end of a career. Chapter 15 covers off the topic of in the moment focus, and what you need to do in order to develop and then retain such a focus from a bout's start to finish.

A DEBRIEFING STRATEGY

One of the consistent themes that resurface in this book is the topic of boxer adaptation. Boxers are always works in progress from the moment they begin to train until the day they choose to stop pursuing an athletic career. Many a talented boxer has traveled through an entire amateur and professional boxing career without a detailed – in-depth understanding of what makes them tick as a competitor. The questions of "why" and how" always creep into every boxer's mind, with only some boxers really knowing why it is they perform as they do, and equally important, how to re-create their peak performances time and again. In my early days working with amateur boxers, I worked with one boxer who was profoundly talented. That boxer would win one high profile tournament and then be eliminated in the first round of the next tournament by a lesser opponent. Part of what I tried to do with that boxer was to have him identify and contrast the differences between his successful tournaments and those where he under-achieved. That athlete never reached his potential, only because he chose not to self-evaluate his performances from one tournament to the next. The athlete went through an entire amateur career without an understanding of what led to better and worse performance for him.

A boxer's understanding is not a matter of guesswork, though some journey through entire boxing careers relying on guesswork. How possibly can you achieve your potential if you do not consider the reasons for each performance shortly after it is experienced? The most successful clients I work with engage in thorough debriefings after their performance. The debriefing begins within 24 hours post-bout, even for athletes earning more than a million dollars for a fight. Every athlete must make time to learn about all of the minute details that explain a better versus a weaker night's work in the ring. With a growing understanding of what makes you tick as a performer, you can then approach the following fight knowing as opposed to believing in your capacities and how those capacities are re-created time and again. Though self-belief/self-confidence is important, even better yet is self-knowledge, built from facts. Knowledge is acquired over time, and a lot of what you can learn as a boxer is gained through correct and thoughtful debriefing sessions with your working team. Have you ever learned something during a bout, only to re-learn it again several months later in another bout? The decision to debrief after fights, and even after important days of sparring or general training will move you forward efficiently toward boxing excellence. Chapter 15 is devoted exclusively to the topic of debriefing. The reason why this chapter ends the substantive content for the book is because I believe it needs to be my parting words to you. Reflection always leads to progression, providing you ask the right questions and then learn from the questions you have asked. Also, remember that the end of each performance needs to be the start and progression forward toward the next performance.

FINAL REFLECTIONS

When you add up the pieces that need to be crafted as part of your mental game plan, several different responses could happen. One possibility is that you look to the components we will discuss and see that there is some work to be done, but that the work is manageable. A second response that might just happen is that you initially become over-whelmed by the number of places where you can make improvements in your mental game plan. A third option response might be that you throw up your hands and so "this is too much work, why bother?" The decision you make to either engage with or disengage from the development of a mental edge, I promise, will be critical to whether you develop as a boxer, how long it takes you to achieve your goals, and how long you are able to sustain your development as a student of the sport.

The reflection I hope you will have is that there are many small places to acquire, that I regard as "crumbs". Each crumb in itself reflects a small amount of energy and investment on your part. Boxing performances are built from lots of small crumbs packaged together. Excellence is built from detail and so you need to be a details person. Detail in terms of how you develop goals leads to a wisely chosen direction. Detail in terms of positive solution oriented thinking leads to persistence so that you achieve your goals – goals don't just happen. Focus in training serves as a sort of quality assurance test that you are pressing your goals into action each day and directing your thinking to where it needs to be – meaning in the moment! Along the way, you need to share all of the above with your working team, including your coach, and possibly a few of the following: a strength and conditioning person, a nutritionist, your personal family / sport doctor, and yes, your sport psychology resource person. When engaging in your discussions with the people who support you, the sharing of ideas, concerns, and solutions needs to be open and continuous. Only with communication is it possible to develop and maintain a shared vision that stands the test of a formidable opponent and tournament opportunity.

Next, there are several chronological pieces for you to install as part of a larger performance plan. Now obviously some of what you need to work on addresses self-awareness and so, what you need to do leading up to the performance. Another critical piece of the puzzle is your understanding of your opponent, and also, the performance environment you will box in. Understanding well in advance of the performance is what I suggest to all of my clients. Behind my approach to longer-term understanding is the realization that boxers need to feel comfortable with the aspects needed in their performance if they are to really use them effectively in the ring. Athletes who tackle understanding entirely, or mostly, in the moment, often become over-whelmed by the immense information that requires processing. You need time to understand the challenges before you, and that takes planning.

The final point we need to agree on is that you are committed to your development as a boxer. Some of that development and evolution requires that you continue to learn about yourself and then put what you have learned into action. Your commitment to action and growth over time will be what differentiates you from most other boxers out there in the sport, with a few exceptions. Far too often, boxers stall out their progress by trying to maintain skills and results that have gained them success in the past. You need to journey the path less traveled and continue to evolve as a boxer. The skills we have outlined in this chapter speak to a few places you can look into and learn from.

Chapter 4

DEVELOPING YOUR GOALS AND PRESSING THEM INTO ACTION

Every boxer needs a direction – somewhere he/she would like to journey toward as an athlete. Too often we sell ourselves short when we envision our future accomplishments, by making our goals overly soft or vague. Boxing is riddled with journeymen who misspend their youth developing their technical skills, though not an understanding of where those skills might take them. It is common for me to hear clients early on in a consulting contract discussing general hopes for their boxing development. Some boxers wish to be better performers, others wish to be world class, and still others aspire to be world champions. What makes one athlete's goals better than another's? Rest assured that the person who develops and revises his goals correctly and also, consistently, has a much more efficient journey to the upper boundaries of his capacities – boundaries that often even surprise the athlete.

One of the elite professional boxers I encountered recently while working with a client in a training camp has been a professional boxer for more than 10 years. Despite his years in, the boxer only recently was able to fight for a world title, and unfortunately the outcome was a loss. The boxer is now well into his 30s and in the final year or two of his career. How is it that a world-class athlete with a significant amateur pedigree wandered through more than 10 years of a professional career without a clear focus of where he was going and also, how long it should take him to get there? While that athlete was part of my client's training camp, I found myself frustrated by his poor choices and unfocused approach to what could have been an illustrious long-term professional career – one he was capable of achieving. Many times, boxers squander their talent through poor career choices and mismanagement. At the bottom of those choices is often a lack of clear goals to pursue.

In the very same training camp, there sat my client – a boxer who is an emerging power on the global boxing scene today. My client is almost 10 years younger than the athlete I have spoken about directly above. He, also, has a solid amateur pedigree and all of the talent a boxer can hope for. Unlike the aged boxer, my client surrounded himself with an excellent and collaborative working team, who all pull together and help the athlete to plot every step of his career from one bout to the next. With every success and accumulated belt, my client is now looking at the possibilities that are before him, and he chooses among those possibilities, wisely and progressively. The world is his oyster, partly because of a vision he and those around him held for his prospects.

It is no accident that one boxer has experienced an escalated rise to the top where the other has yet to fulfill his potential despite their significant difference in age. This chapter is not just about objectives for one point in time. Understand that goals are set for periods of time, and each series of goals is meant to connect in almost a linear way with the goals that come after it, as well as the goals that came before it. Athletic visions must be built with lots of thought and reflection, and not as "one offs" to last onward for eternity. So back to my earlier question: how is it that an athlete might squander away an entire professional career? The answer is quite simple: mental laziness and a lack of forethought in terms of how the technical, tactical, and psychological pieces of the athlete's development must blend into a larger performance visions over time. Though you might not believe it, through a correct and well-conceived vision you can surpass many of the more talented and experienced athletes you have yet to encounter. Though talent is important, it is also over-rated and squandered by even some of the most promising and gifted boxers on the scene, today. My client's sparring partner was one such example of a career delayed and perhaps blocked by lack of goal-directed thinking.

SETTING YOUR VISION

When we listen to the words of emerging boxers, just stepping onto the global scene today, most have shared that their vision as a boxer stems from hopes and dreams started early in their life. Recently, while watching Fight Club 360 on ShowTime, I listened to Alan Green describe his childhood and how he always walked around thinking of Sugar Ray Robinson. Others such as Jean Pascal have identified Roy Jones Jr. as their role model. Though the assignment of a role model is not really the focus of our discussion, for many a boxer, role models were the motivation that brought and sometimes kept them in the sport. Likely each and every world class athlete in his youth was able to replace the role model with his own name and identity as the young aspiring boxer began to dream of excellence.

Visions begin early in a boxer's development. Even though the vision might start with the reference to a role model, soon that vision contains only the athlete and where he sees himself going in, though also, through sport. Your vision is meant to contain in part your athletic identity, but also your more general identity as a professional, friend, and family person. Though you likely have a well-formed vision, let's see if we can fill in the details and even add some additional culture and definition.

As an athlete, you likely (and hopefully) see yourself as an accomplished boxer, with as much success as you dare to consider. Do you also see what you look like in the ring? What style of performer are you? Do you have a philosophy in the ring? What is your emotional state as you engage in battle? Can you see yourself slowly or all at once taking the control of the ring, the opponent, the judges, and even the audience?

Now let's discuss how you envision yourself as a boxer more generally. What do you see as your work ethic each day in training? Do you approach each day's training with enthusiasm? What is your relationship with your coach? Do you have lots of good friends in the gym who you support, and who also in exchange, support you? What sort of coaching and sport science staff surrounds you? How do you generally feel about being a boxer?

Wider yet, how do you see your life outside of the ring? Are you a student? If so, what sort of subjects are you focusing on? How are your grades? If you aren't a student and instead, you have a job outside of boxing, what sort of job do you have? What is your projected salary? How is your personal life? Where do you live? Who do you live with?

All of the questions above are examples of aspects that need to be written into your vision. Take 45 minutes, sit down, and write a vision for yourself on paper. The vision can address who you will be two, five, or ten years from today. Write the entire vision onto one piece of paper and don't be skimpy in terms of who you are. What I mean is that you should write about your vision as if it was already achieved and you are presently living your dream.

Each morning you need to read that sheet and start the day off with a reminder of what your vision is, and so, where you are moving toward. Having a vision is a powerful motivational tool and strategy. Visions keep you on track with your ultimate ambitions by keeping you focused toward to correct direction. Far too often people wander through their days with little thought of where they are going, and far too much focus only on the immediate. The immediate is a reality, but so too, your vision can become a reality so long as you continue to think in the right direction and from that thinking, make great decisions.

THE IMPORTANCE OF GOAL SUPPORTIVE TEAMS

The picture of goal-directedness would be incomplete if we did not also think about the influence of coaches among a few other supportive influences that surround most every boxer. Sometimes, a boxer's career is rescued by a progressive working team. Recently, a boxer I am beginning to work with was on the precipice of either making it to the top of his game, or failing out of the sport entirely. The boxer's record suggests that he is indeed a talented athlete. With more than 20 professional wins and no losses to his name the athlete is touted as an emerging prospect in his weight division, so much so that most every major sports network would like to underwrite his fights – at least for now.

There is little doubt that the athlete is happy with his success and also, that he has the necessary confidence in his skills and abilities. And yet, there has been something desperately missing within the athlete. His motivation to train declined recently, he seems unhappy with his coaching and managerial staff, and from what I see, the athlete is in need of some support – in a very specific way. That support must be offered in terms of a candid discussion regarding the efforts he needs to exert in training and how those efforts will translate into even better performance. A prospect's past accomplishments are indeed inspiring, but not near as inspiring as the potential accomplishments that are before him in the future. A clear and well-developed roadmap to the future must also connect with the present or the consequence is that an athlete's career stalls out due to an uninspired approach.

Even for the most talented and capable of boxers, a focus or re-focus on goals needs to be taken with every performance. The trick is to act progressively so that goals are re-set at crucial times in a boxer's development, to sustain effort and not remedy its decline. The wonderful end to the story is that the athlete's working team is now starting to pull together, and I would expect that a remedy to the athlete's lack of focus is at hand. Equally critical, the boxer and his team need to recognize from this point onward, the importance of moving forward with incremental goals that remind the athlete of the pathway he has chosen and where it might, and hopefully will, lead him. In conjunction with that pathway, specific commitments need to be made in terms of training intensity and also, a solution oriented approach.

PROCESS AND OUTCOME GOALS

Now let's look more closely at the boxer discussed directly above. One might wonder whether he lacked direction entirely as he progressed deeper into his boxing career. From what little I know of the athlete at present, he has been focused on developing a lucrative boxing career. His KO percentage is amazing and he feels that his list of victims will grow. I am going to speculate that if I were to ask the athlete about his view of himself as a boxer presently, he feels that he can knock out most any opponent right away. He might also say that he is ready for his first big pay day, all that needs to happen is that he needs the opponent placed in front of him. Perhaps this young lion is correct – he might be ready, but I believe that at the heart of what needs to be tidied is a differentiation between process and outcome oriented goals.

Every indication is that the athlete has bought into immediate gratification in the form of successful results. The athlete's boxing record reflects an orientation almost exclusively to outcomes. Little does the athletes understand that in order to sustain a lucrative career, or any boxing evolution, there must be a balance of outcome and process oriented goals. Outcome goals are exactly what they sound like – the focus is on winning, numbers, dollars, and exposure. If you comb through the interviews of long-standing champion pugilists, you will find that they also refer to somewhat of a process orientation. What I mean is that they understand very clearly what sorts of decisions day in and day out in training, and also within each fight, must happen in order for the athlete to achieve the favorable outcomes he/she seeks. A focus on outcomes with a balanced understanding of the journey along the way is a focus devoted to flash and not to the nitty gritty details that produce that flash, from one boxing opportunity to the next.

So what do you think needs to happen when you set your goals? Well, the outcome goals are meant to inspire you and also to serve as guideposts that you are moving in the direction you have charted for your boxing. Outcome goals are important because without them, there is really no finish line that marks the accomplishment of the goal in a tangible way. What I always propose is that when boxers set their goals, they start with the outcome – target and declare it. What I mean is that the outcome goal needs to be written on paper and then posted in your room. Then, to move toward your target you need to consider the essential things you need to develop while working in the trenches toward your outcome. One example might be boxing with a complete focus within each round of sparring or a fight, from the bell that marks the start of the round to the bell that marks its end (remembering to always protect yourself).

So, back to the young lion I have written about above, at least one of his process goals needs to be devoted to an unwavering – relentless, positive and energetic approach to training in advance of each fight. As the athlete goes deeper into his career, he must soon realize that the results he will gain against the top athletes in his division will come as a result of sufficient hard work over a reasonable amount of time, in advance of each bout, and not just in the ring. Boxers often forget the work in the trenches and you must remember that a good process connects with a great outcome.

GOALS AND HOW TO DEVELOP THEM

The importance of setting your goals is immense. With well-designed goals, people can inch forward in progress and slowly, achieve great objectives. Though any motivational book has a section devoted exclusive to goals, still, even those who read such books struggle to set and re-set effective goals. There are specific and well-established criteria that you need to keep in the back of your mind if you really want to either set new goals or consider the goals you have set recently. The acronym, meaning the abbreviation for the list of criteria are often referred to in the business of sport psychology as SMART goals. The word SMART stands for (1) Specific, (2) Measurable, (3) Achievable, (4) Relevant, and (5) Time-based. Below we need to look more closely at the five goal-setting criteria in order to avoid most every mistake that even the best boxers commit when they set their goals.

Specific

Take the criteria "specific". You likely remember that earlier in the book I spoke about boxers who aspire to be "great" or "the best" they can be. With both examples it is easy to understand why some athletes commit the mistake of being overly general in their objectives. Goals need to be defined. Reaching your potential is a great ambition, but really, what does that potential really mean? Does is signify becoming a world champion, a *RING* Champion, a national champion, a Golden or Silver Gloves Champion, or something else that is very specific? The point I am trying to make is that goals need to be as specific as you can make them, and there is no such thing as too specific. Far too often I witness amateur and professional boxers at the elite level wander their way through their boxing opportunities without a very specific objective. Should you choose to be more specific than most, you will then define yourself as different and likely you will surpass all those generalists (people who set general instead of specific goals).

Measurable

Goals also must be measurable when you set them. How do you know where the start and finish lines for a given goal are if you do not also integrate measurement? One example that a few of my clients have used in professional boxing has been to box a complete three minutes of every round from bell to bell. There is no mistaking whether a boxer keeps his focus for the entire round. The boxers who do stay in the fight and usually outlast their opponents. So few boxers maintain a consistent focus. When you anchor the criteria of time to the goal it is truly measurable – either the boxer stayed engaged for three minutes or he didn't – it's just that simple. How often can you find an athlete boxing a brilliant round only to lose his focus for a few second – the same few seconds when he is caught by a temple or a body shot that staggers. I recall not long ago, one of my clients was fighting a fantastic bout and upsetting his opponent in a world title bout (the opponent was the reigning champion). In the fifth round my client was fighting perhaps his most complete round, and he became extremely taken with the fact that things were unfolding even better than he could have imagined in advance of the encounter. With about thirty seconds remaining in the round, my client was caught with a temple shot – as he explained later, because his concentration lapsed. My client survived the round and also won a unanimous decision. He fought 11+ rounds with concentration. However, that one lapse of concentration inside the parameters of a three-minute round almost cost him a world title! So, the importance of adding time to an athlete's objective of solid concentration is a good decision.

Achievable

When you set goals, your intent is to reach – achieve them. Many a time boxers set their goals, well below a standard they should be considering. Soft / easy goals will keep you in the comfort zone, and they might even maintain a reasonable standard of success. The boxing world has met a few elite professional athletes who've chosen their opponents so wisely that they have retained their titles, but at the same time, they have stalled out a career – their career. The sad thing about such athletes as that by choosing soft goals, or in this case, successive soft opponents, they lose all confidence in what they are really capable of. Satisfaction in boxing comes from pushing yourself ever so slightly out of the comfort zone, though on a regular basis. Without tests along the way, we never really know what we are made of. And so, soft goals take away from confidence, and sadly, they result in unsatisfying experiences in the sport.

The question becomes how do you know what is achievable from what isn't? There is no easy answer to the question, but one thing is for certain: you need to arrive at that conclusion with the assistance of someone who knows boxing and is also, trustworthy. Together, you need to consider what your capabilities are and then having agreed on what a reasonable stretch is, go after your goal. Not long ago, I was part of a working team where a boxer wasn't sure of whether he had the stuff to defeat a reigning world champion in his weight division. At a certain point in the discussion, the athlete became so enthused by the belief of his well-established team that he agreed to accept the fight. A few months later, he won the bout and the rest has since become history.

Relevant

When you set your goals they must also be relevant to you! I recall once in my early days as a consultant when a wonderfully accomplished amateur athlete and I worked closely together. The athlete had won medals at most every major international boxing tournament, including several major games competitions. The athlete was a truly gifted athlete, and everyone including his coach knew and appreciated his talent and also, his potential. As the Olympics drew near the athlete was considering his prospects after the monumental tournament that was fast approaching.

Looking past an immediate tournament is always something I have encouraged my elite clients to do. As this athlete was looking to where he might wish to go after the Olympics, discussions were directed toward a professional career away from elite sport. The athlete was also university educated, and he was as gifted in his educational trajectory as he was in sport. The challenge my client encountered, however, was that his coach had different dreams for the athlete, starting with an illustrious professional boxing career. The coach's objective was to prepare his athlete for that professional career and in the meantime, land the athlete a hefty signing bonus.

For the athlete, the concept of becoming a professional boxer was not enticing, and so, not relevant. You would be surprised how often a relevant goal in the eyes of an athlete might not be a relevant goal from the standpoint of his/he coach. Often, boxers know what is a relevant goal to them, and so as an athlete, you must lead any discussion that pertains to your goals. On the other hand, in my humble opinion, it is also important to resource the coaches who train you and seek feedback about your goals, especially if you are looking to progress to the next level of boxing. Remember, there are times like the example above where athletes draw the line and know whether the relevance and direction of a goal makes sense. However, there are also other times such as in the aged boxer we discussed a few pages ago where a strong – directive team could have assisted the athlete in determining good career decisions, given that they could have led to a relevant outcome in the eyes of the athlete.

Time-based

Last but not least, you need to anchor your goals to a time frame. Say for example you are a highly successful amateur boxer, performing in the US. Your goal might be to eventually make the United States National Boxing Team. Ok, that sounds like an inspiring goal, especially if you have shown your worth in Golden Gloves Competitions and you have medaled at a recent national championships. But, when do you wish to gain your birth onto the national team? Remember that people do age out of goals, and sometimes, those who fall short meet all of the other goal-setting criteria discussed just above, but one. Where they lose their focus and miss the mark is by failing to realize that every goal has an expiry date that comes with it.

Consider a professional athlete who wishes to become a world champion. I am certain you and I have watched many of those athletes on most every sports network that features elite level prize fighting. For some pugilists the goal of becoming king is always a goal somewhere in the distance – on the horizon. The reality is that among most professional boxers, the peak years are from 26-32 years of age. So, if they turn professional at age 19-20, they only have six or seven years to reach the top of the rankings and only several attempts at world titles and title defenses. There is nothing more sad than a shop worn fighter still seeking out goals that he should have chased down much earlier, in a more time urgent way.

So, set a data to your goal. A national team aspirant might say that he is the 2011 US Heavyweight champion. The professional aspirants I work with set a date when they are shooting for a belt. For example, one athlete might say on the night of December 21, 2011, I am the International Boxing Federation's Super Middleweight Champion. You will notice that the time is specific, and also, that I ask my clients to own their goals by re-stating them as "I am statements".

Developing Your Goals into Affirmations

Some years ago I began working with clients on their "I am" statements. I also refer to "the statements" as positive self-affirmations. The agenda is to have the athlete take his/her goals and re-word them as if they already exist, and also as if they are part of the athlete's identity. Athletes, much like every other type of performer, train in their sport each day, with all kinds of interesting self-talk going on. Self-talk is an unavoidable part of what happens in your mind, during training and also in competition. There is no reason to stop the chatter that happens. My suggestion always is to make the chatter positive and more than just positive, constructive. In fact, if you read Chapter Seven you will see that it is devoted entirely to the topic of self-talk and positive thinking. The reason why originates with extensive research about the power of internal and spoken language, meaning the language you say to yourself, and also, the language you share with others. In this section, we will tackle self-affirmations. You need to systematically develop a strategy with positive and constructive self-talk. Remember, being positive is great, but if optimism does not also tie in tangible thinking, it is just fluff.

The "I am" statements that we are about to work through are an opportunity for you to develop statements about yourself that focus you on where you are going. Simply follow what I suggest below for a minimum of two weeks and I promise, you will see a big difference to the positive in how you view yourself as a boxer.

Some years ago, I worked with Canada's National Women's Boxing Team in advance of the World Championships. One of the workshops we did right off the bat was self-affirmations. I began with an explanation of all of the mechanics required for effective goal-setting. We spoke about SMART goals, about process and outcome goals, and we also spoke about the importance of declaring who we are – something that you, also, need to do. When we got down to the task of working, I asked each boxer to develop four goals for the upcoming World Championship. That year's World Championship was the target. I asked that 1-2 of the goals address what they needed to do in terms of process outside and inside the ring in order to be at their best. One girl mentioned that she needed to be very well organized and throughout the tournament, to stick to a self-care schedule. Housed within the goal were lots of sleep, good hydration, good nutrition, relaxation time, and a good performance plan. So, "being organized" became one of the athlete's four goals. Another athlete piped in and said that she needed to stay focused on scoring points and maintaining a good defense for every second of every round until the bout ended in success. Both of the examples just described were process goals that were essential to every boxer. For the athlete who previously let go of her structure during international tournaments however, the focus on staying within her structure was essential. For the athlete who needed to stay focused, there was a previous tendency to lose focus and allow he mind to wander – something she was going to remedy at the World Championships in two weeks time.

Each athlete was also asked to develop an outcome goal as her last goal in the session. I recall most athletes identifying that they were going to be medalists at that year's World Championships. One athlete in particular declared boldly during the session that she was going to win the gold medal. I could see that the athlete meant what she said, and the athlete's belief was confirmed when later she was the first athlete to post her goals on the front of her door – for all of the other athletes and staff to see.

Once the women developed their goals, they re-wrote them as "I am statements", meaning every goal had to start with the words I am... We made certain the goals met the standards set out above by reviewing each athlete's goals very carefully. Then, the athletes were asked to post their list of goals on the inside and outside of the door to their room, by their bed, in their equipment bag, and by their work desk. Every time each athlete walked by her goals, she was tasked with reading them. Though some focused people do think about their objectives a few times a day, these girls landed up reading their goals 30-40 times each day for a span of two weeks before they departed to the competition. Further, the women were tasked with re-posting their goals when they arrived at the competition, in the very same places.

The first athlete to post her goals was ahead of all of the other boxers by at least one day. However, soon, all of the athletes moved beyond the initial embarrassment or concern of being embarrassed by others, and before long all in essence, declared their objectives and what needed to be done. All of the athletes also declared that they were going to medal. You will never guess what happened at the World Championships? All of the women medaled and the most aggressive athlete in posting her goals became the first Canadian Women's World Champion.

The thing is that you need to know where you are going every day, and not just on occasion when asked. You need to declare to yourself who you are and where you are moving – you need a good direction, and that direction needs to be understood as often as you dare consider it. Boxers have lots of self-talk happening before, during, and after training. I think that you need to develop the right focus, and the chatter that you engage in has got to be well-developed chatter so that you continue to move in the right direction. So, develop your affirmations, and declare them quickly – there is not a moment to waste.

FINAL REFLECTIONS

There are lots of ways to go about goal-setting strategies. In this chapter you have some of the basics to get you started. You need to tackle your goals, and tackle them regularly. There will likely be some goals that have some immediacy to them. Remember, much like the young prospect that I wrote about earlier in this chapter, the decisions you are making in the short-term need to connect with long-term success. Goals are meant to ensure that you think about your future, and that you don't let that future slip away much like the aged athlete I also spoke about at the beginning of this chapter. You need to set a course for yourself and that course needs to integrate the SMART criteria that we spoke about a few pages ago.

There is also something very important that you need to consider when developing your goals: you need to develop them in collaboration with the coaches who work with you. Remember that you might think a certain goal is challenging, and in some cases, even the best athletes sell themselves short. Be different, work on your goals, and work on them collaboratively with your working team.

Once you set your goals, you also have to post them, and by posting them, you are declaring your direction to yourself and the people who matter most. Engage in the project of developing your affirmations, and do it quickly. Why postpone your future – every day is spent either in focus or it is squandered. You never know what one more day of focus might do in terms of your boxing evolution. Through focus come good decisions, and on a given day, that extra day where you were goal-directed, you might learn something amazing that can serve you well not only today, but also, every other day that follows today.

Chapter 5

TRAINING DELIBERATELY

When you look through most every book about sport psychology there is a chapter devoted entirely to athlete focus, or athlete concentration. In many ways these two terms address the very same underlying topic, where the emphasis is devoted to being in the present. From the hours I have spent observing boxers, and I have spent many hours in gyms observing boxers, it often appears to me that most are not focused on the present. Boxers shadow box in front of mirrors without much focus, and they also mentally wander through their skipping rope. It seems to me that for many boxers, focus is required only (or at least mostly) for pad work and sparring.

If we take a step back from the general practice of warming into a training session as described above, I always wonder whether focus in training should not be committed to from much earlier on the workout and then extend to the warming down phase of training, also. If an athlete devotes 2-3 hours in an afternoon to training and only 45-60 minutes of that training reflects a complete focus, I find such an approach terribly inefficient. After all, from extensive research with athletes and experts in many other domains, it takes a minimum of 10,000 hours of concentrated practice in order to become an accomplished performer. When you squander away 2/3 of your training session to a lack of focus, you are physically training, but you definitely are not training with deliberate – in the moment focus.

In the present chapter we need to consider much more closely the topic of deliberate focus. Though you might not realize it, if you invest all of your focus into every moment of training, you will progress much quicker as a boxer than the person who only focuses during moments that he/she views as crucial moments. I mentioned earlier on that athletes only have a finite number of hours in which to perfect their training. Those hours are reflected in a fixed number of years, after which boxers lose their speed and then eventually, their power.

When you attack your training with enthusiasm and a commitment to entire focus each and every day, you are actually taking the very first step toward speeding up your progression. Remember, it is not only a matter of "hours invested" in training, but also, the investment you make when you are physically engaged in your gym time. Next, we are going to look very closely at how to train deliberately. You might be one of the few boxers who do train deliberately from the beginning to the end of each session, and if so, this chapter will confirm that you are on the correct track. On the other hand, in more cases than not, by reading this chapter you will also pick up a few helpful hints of how to tighten your focus in training so that you increase the benefit of what you gain from each and every session, physically and also, mentally. As a parting shot, know that only through complete mental focus can you gain the full benefit from the physical training your coach has structured for you today, and tomorrow.

THE TRAINING COMMITMENT

Your decision to engage in training is more than just a general commitment to attend training each day - your engagement must be a deliberate – intentional engagement. Your complete and full attention with a day's training doesn't just happen because you have decided to be more attentive each day. You need to consider first how focused you have been in past sessions. If you believe you have been completely focused, look and see whether there are minutes you have squandered each day as you have wandered through what have become the habitual processes of a day's training.

Think about the following questions and answer them with brutal honesty: do you set goals before you step into the gym each day regarding that day's training? As you are getting changed into your training gear, do you think about your objectives and remind yourself of your training objectives for the day and also, your commitment to a complete focus? As you start skipping rope, are you in the present focusing on the rope, keeping a good rhythm, and moving your feet out of the way of the rope as it passes by your feet? When you start your shadow boxing, do you choose an opponent and really think about a strategy implementation, or do you just go through the motions? If you are focusing on yourself in the mirror, do you look closely at your technique to ensure you are doing all of the correct things your coach has been reinforcing? How about when you hit the heavy bag or medicine bag? Are you considering the sorts of punches you need to throw? Are you moving your feet? Are you pushing yourself physically? How about when you step into the ring for technical sparring? Are you committed to a full three minutes of focus from the beginning to the end of each round? Are you implementing the tactics you and your coach have discussed in relation to the boxer in front of you?

You get the idea- few are the boxers who are really in the moment during a day's training. If you choose the path of mindlessness during training, you will progress aimlessly through your development as a boxer. You will progress to a certain degree through general training. However, with a complete focus in your training, you will gain all of the correct habits over time, by making the appropriate decisions within every day's training. You need to bank each day's training as one more day with a complete focus. Through a habit of concentration, you will gain all of the best habits, and you will gain them quickly. Then, when you encounter a tough test in the ring, you can guess what sorts of skills will surface when you need them most. Travel the road less traveled and engage in a complete focus, each day. Also, from time to time, look around you and notice the boxers who are just wandering their way through that day's training. You will be surprised of what you notice. Good boxers surpass more talented boxers by banking the correct decisions each day. Invest in your boxing future and commit to a complete, and not a half-hearted focus.

COMMITTING BEFORE YOU WALK INTO THE GYM

Ok, so what is your objective for today? Do you know what the structure for today's training is? If so, have you set a few specific goals for yourself? If you are training in the afternoon, either after school or a day on the job, this initial step of your commitment to deliberate focus should start in the morning while you are waking up and having your breakfast. It is better to set a goal immediately before you walk into the gym, or as you are walking into the gym, than not setting a goal at all. However, if you start thinking about your commitment to today's training earlier in the day, you have much more time to really think about what you are looking to achieve.

Once you've set your focus for today's training, re-visit the idea throughout the day. Recently, I worked with a National Hockey League player, who was in training camp with a high profile NHL team. The athlete and I began working together during the beginning of a week's training camp. At the end of the training camp, the coaching staff had to choose its final selection of players for the year – its team members. The first day we spoke about deliberate attention and being solution oriented during every drill. The commitment was for the athlete to make quick decisions and to trust in the years of training he banked to that point in his playing career. The athlete also committed to responding positively after a mistake and making a better decision immediately after the error he just made. You will see that in Chapter Seven (two chapters from now) we will discuss positive and constructive thinking in detail. However, for the sake of deliberate focus, I wanted the athlete to be in the present, and committed to acting and reacting very quickly, relying on his years of experience and intuition. That day, the athlete surpassed everyone's expectations and showed some brilliance. For the athlete to be so intuitive, we had to discuss his game plan for the day's training, the night before. It actually took the athlete nearly 24 hours to develop and then press his plan into action.

The following day, I didn't hear from the athlete. After the fact I learned that his performance went down. When we debriefed late the night after the weak day's performance it was very clear that the athlete approached the second day's training mindlessly, without a well-developed plan before he engaged in the training session. So, we returned to the concept of brainstorming and came up with a battle plan for the third day's training. During the third day's training the athlete went upward in performance, and that day's performance was his best in the camp to date.

Even with good professional athletes, training is often approached with an inconsistent strategy, and sometimes, no strategy at all. Though you may think a day's focus doesn't make much of a difference, I am here to tell you that it does make a difference! Each day of great training serves as the foundation you need to place trust in during crucial moments of a performance. When you have piled up lots of hours of good decisions, built from a commitment to a deliberate focus, you gain confidence in your development. After all, much like the captain of a ship, you have learned how to chart a course and then, to set sail.

Now back to the NHL prospect, he sadly did not make his team. You needn't wonder why. The reason for the athlete's de-selection was most likely inconsistent performance. Only through consistent performance can you and your coach build a solid sense of belief in your capacities as a boxer. So, you need to develop your objectives for each day's training, much like you need to have a specific plan for each opponent. Plan's need forethought – meaning a clear idea of what needs to be accomplished in advance of every day's performance. Set your plan for each day's training early on each morning, or even the night before the following day's training.

WALKING INTO THE GYM

To engage in deliberate practice, you must connect your training objectives, set earlier in the day, with where you are presently at – entering into the gym. There is always a distinction between talking the talk and walking the walk. As you enter into the gym, it is your opportunity to walk the walk, in relation to the day's training goals. Most athletes enter the gym without much thought about what they would like to achieve that day. Why not press your focus into action by returning to your objectives as you actually walk into the gym.

First thing you need to do is open your shoulders and approach the training facility with conviction. Posture plays an important role in the attitude you take and the focus you have when stepping into the training environment. By opening your shoulders and pushing out your chest a little, you reinforce to yourself the idea that you have arrived at the gym and that you are ready to tackle a tough day's training. There is an old saying that people need to "step up" when they face a challenge. Each day, you need to step up and attack your training with energy and commitment.

Imagine what would happen if you committed to physically engaging in training each day as you entered the training environment? You would gain much more benefit from your training and you would make each session count in a profound way. Few and far between are the athletes who step up in training each day – and I am telling you that one big difference that separates the good from the great is that capacity to step up each day. Stepping up doesn't just happen as you enter into the ring and start a sparring session. Stepping up begins early in the morning of each day as you commit to that day's goals, and then it extends throughout the day and into the moments when you step in to the gym. So, commit to stepping up as you walk into the gym.

Remember, open up your shoulders, make your walk a little more aggressive, think about what it is that you are looking to achieve today, and then commit to yourself that you will press those ideas into action. Pressing ideas into action obviously requires some positive self-talk, which we will discuss a little more in the chapter after next. However, for now, the ideas and words that should be running through your self-talk should focus entirely on what you have planned for today's training and what you need to do to live up to your day's vision.

When you dare to think deliberately about what you are looking for in terms of performance, you open yourself up to possibilities that many other boxers likely don't even consider on a daily basis. Far too often, people wander into their training session and coast through the day's activities as if they are something that must be pushed through. Take a much more aggressive and constructive approach, and dare to walk the walk each day as you enter into your training. Doing so is much like investing a penny in the bank, each day. Before you know it, you will have banked many days of amazing training, all the while developing a habit of hardened focus that you will automatically carry with you into the ring. What you do intentionally becomes what you do unintentionally. Harden your approach as you walk into the gym.

PUSHING YOUR TRAINING FORWARD WHILE GETTING DRESSED

Many of the boxers I have met along the way enter into the gym in their jeans, say hello to their training partners and friends, and then get changed for the day's training. If you follow the same procedure dressing is actually also meant to be a step toward a deliberate day's training. I will bet that as you get dressed for a day's training session you likely don't give much thought to anything other than simply putting on your shorts and shirt, wrapping your hands, and tying your boots. Makes sense to me, those are the things you typically do, so why attend to more than the basics?

Well, there is more to dressing than some boxers realize. First and foremost, the clothes you wear need to confirm who you are as a boxer. If you are wearing clothes that are sloppy and poor quality, what do you think you will eventually see in the mirror when you skip rope and then start your shadow boxing? What you see is what you get. The way you look needs to be professional and so, motivational. Some years ago, I was a national team member in another sport. I was fortunate enough to work with a highly successful Olympic coach – a fellow who was a former Olympic Gold medalist and also a multiple time Olympic Gold Medal coach. When that coach started working with the national team I was part of, the first lesson he taught us all was that we needed to look the part. Before long we all arrived at each day's training much like a person in business dresses for her/his job. Just by dressing for the task, we slowly shifted out focus a little closer to what the task was going to be that day. Remember, the way you present will impact on the way you feel and how you will behave in training.

Next, dressing requires some attention to detail. I have found many a time that boxers need to re-wrap their hands, or retie their shoelaces, or tighten their gloves part way through a day's training. To me it is obvious that such people were not attending to the details of dressing when they should have – before they started their physical warm-up. The moment such athletes have to correct and adjust their equipment, they have also taken themselves out of the rhythm and focus if training. There is nothing wrong with deliberately training yourself to adjust for in the moment equipment challenges, where you need to keep your focus while your coach tightens or re-tapes a glove. However, if you are not seeking to train that aspect within today's training, it should not become a distraction from today's training flow.

What you need to do is pay attention to the details associated with dressing as you are dressing, and not after the fact. Pay now or pay later, as the saying goes. My suggestion is that when you are putting on your training wraps, focus on the tension and distribution of weight while you are wrapping. When you are tying your shoelaces, again, be in the moment, set the right tension and then double tie the laces. If you need to, also tape the laces. When putting on your gloves, again, push your hand fully into the glove and then direct the person tying the laces or pulling the Velcro in terms of the perfect tension.

Once you have taken the slow and precise steps of putting on your equipment, you will automatically feel ready – prepared for today's training. As you can see, you don't just cruise into a day's training session and expect a complete focus. If you are a person who cruises into a day's training, you are leaving the focus and quality of that days training up to the luck of the day. On the other hand, if you choose the correct pathways to preparing, stepping into the gym, and then dressing for training, you will be up for the task. Far too often talented athletes lack the professional approach expected of most every other professional person who goes off to the office. The boxing gym is your office. Dress professionally and be mindful of how you dress so that you are free to put your entire focus into today's training.

WARMING UP AND BUILDING FOR DELIBERATE PRACTICE

Warming up is another opportunity to pay attention to what you are doing today in training. I recall sharing with you that most people typically warm themselves into a day's training. They might even label the day's training their "workout session". There is a distinct difference between working out and training deliberately. Working out reflects a thought process where actually, there often is not much thought at all invested in the training. Working out suggests that you are simply just going through the paces of physical activity, pushing your heart rate, breaking a sweat, and generally, either developing or maintaining boxing fitness. As you will realize in two chapters from now, the way we term each day's training determines the sort of meaning we impose on it and so, what we gain from that day. Remember that each day's training is either a day banked or a day squandered.

Shadow boxing is a prime example of where I sometimes find gross inefficiency in a boxer's focus. I have asked boxers many times what they think during their shadow boxing. Some reply that they don't think at all and only look to break a sweat, or to warm-into their day's training. I agree that shadow boxing is a progressive step found within the warm-up, meant to bring the boxer closer to the specifics of a day's training, as compared with skipping rope, which happens to be a much more general task. In relation to what we have discussed to this point in the immediate chapter though, shadow boxing can be used to build focus in relation to today's objectives. If the goal is to cut off the ring and push the opponent backwards into a corner, than that strategy would logically also belong within shadow boxing. If the goal is to stick and move, then the coach should be able to observe that strategy. By reinforcing today's objectives through shadow boxing, when there is no opponent or coach's pad in front of the athlete, you press your strategy into action within a straight forward, and simple context. Then, with the strategy under your belt, you can then test it and press it into action within an interactive situation, such as when you work with your coach during pad work or when you test the strategy as part of a technical sparring session.

Working on a heavy bag or a medicine bag as part of your training should also be part of the deliberate process we have just considered. For example, when boxers use the heavy bag, many forget to move their legs, and stay in one spot far too long. Staying stationary, especially in the ring, creates a situation even for the most heavy handed of boxers where they can become a sitting duck. Not long ago while working with an athlete overseas as part of a training camp, I watched a world-class coach remind a world champion to move his legs while working out on the heavy bag, and to constantly change the angles he was hitting from. I have known that athlete for some time and always noticed that when he was working on the heavy bag he often stayed in one spot. What you do in training becomes what surfaces in competition, when you are really being tested to the maximum. So, in relation to the heavy bag, the coach correctly reminded the athlete that there are details to be taken to even the most repetitive of tasks.

The challenge in a day's workout is to bring common sense and a systematic approach to a training session, where others would approach that very same session mindlessly. Deliberate practice in training is not only a matter of banking hours in correct decisions and detailed training. A focused approach to training becomes the solid footing that you eventually will stand on in competition. Your knowledge and know how built from deliberate training will take you several steps closer to a profound level of confidence, built with basis as opposed to a general approach to boxing.

PRACTICE IN SPARRING

There is much more to sparring than at first meets the eye. The logic behind correctly structured sparring is for you to integrate aspects from your training in a competition like situation. Arguably, open sparring is closer to a competition like scenario than technical sparring. I have been witness to coaches and athletes engaging in regular sparring, meaning in some cases, an almost equal amount of sparring proportionate to technical drills. I agree that it is important from time to time to structure sparring into your progressive training – but how?

Sparring has a purpose, and that purpose is for you to press into action aspects you have worked on in training at the correct moment, as a tactic. When sparring is structured into a day's training, the intent must be to reinforce the skills you have been working on, and also, to serve as an acid test that those skills are well-integrated as part of your knowledge. After all, who is to know whether you have really integrated skills and that you understand how and when to employ them until a little bit of a challenge is structured into your training? So, sparring serves a purpose, and if it is tied into a larger training regime with care, meaning selectively, it becomes a crucial part of overall learning.

There is a considerable gap between working on a skill in training and then using that skill in the heat of competition. Sparring is the tool that connects training drills with the reality that those skills must be used on an opponent, in the same ring, who also tests what he has been working on in training. With sparring, there needs to be a meaningful transition from technical drills, to the increased challenge of technical sparring (where one encounters an opponent, though without the challenge of full contact), to the very real test of open sparring. To skip from one phase of training to the next too early, you risk the chance of reinforcing undeveloped, or poorly developed skills under pressure, and then missing the positive experience of a confirming performance and the confidence that goes with it. Sparring needs to be used to press skills into action in life-like performance circumstances, and not randomly. Be progressive in how you structure sparring into your training, and use it as a test that all of your skills are in place and that you can count on them to surface when those skills are needed most.

COOLING DOWN AND REINFORCING IDEAS

There are many times in our lives when we study for something, complete the task, and then let the details go. As the saying goes: knowledge in, knowledge out. The approach I am proposing to you is one of mindfulness and being in the present each minute of your training session. How often have you completed the detailed work in your training session and then used your physical cool down as a mental cool down also? Have you ever been witness to a professional boxer who boxed an almost complete bout, only to lose his/her focus in the waning minutes of the fight? I wonder whether the loss of focus for such athletes is something out of the ordinary? My clients always commit to boxing from first bell to final bell with complete focus. I think by now, that message is written into this book loud and clear.

The cool down period is a prime time to work on your focus, especially seeing that you should be a little tired by that point in your day's training. On one level, the cooling down process is an opportunity to reinforce tactics or technical aspects you starting mapping out at the start of the day and then pressed into action within your training. Remember, it is far more efficient to learn things and then integrate what you learn systematically then it is to re-learn things over and over again! On a second level, you need to keep your focus and your cool through discipline, especially when you are tired. The end of a day's training is the perfect opportunity to stay focused and push hard to the very end of that day's training – just as you would in the final few rounds, minutes, or seconds of a bout. Remember that lessons should be transferable from training to performance, with lessons in training always applying to a potential application in the fight.

By developing a late workout focus, and reinforcing that focus toward the end of every workout, you will never have to worry about your focus fading late in the fight. Over the last few years, I have watched a potential Hall of Fame boxer fade in the latter parts of his fight. According to his television interviews, he is under the belief that the late round stoppages he has encountered in the last few fights were a matter of conditioning. That athlete is correct to some degree, though also, not entirely accurate. Though the boxer will remain nameless, and there are several such athletes out there today, I believe that if I were to examine how that athlete trains in the latter parts of every day's workout, I would find that his attention wanders, and it wanders because he has let it wander for far too long. Amazing how poor decisions in training can transfer to career-ending performances. What you practice is exactly what you will do in performance. Make the correct decisions in every day's training from beginning to end and that is exactly what you can anchor your confidence in during the crucial moments of performance.

REMEMBERING THE DETAILS

Much later in this book we will look very closely at the concept of post-bout evaluation. Chapter Fifteen is devoted to the topic of what you can learn from your own performance after the fact. The present chapter has been devoted to the subject of deliberate training, and as part of that training, the very same evaluation process you will eventually consider in relation to competition must now be considered in relation to your training. How often have you learned something about yourself in a day's training, either in terms of something that really worked, or something that you vow never to do again? I will bet you have experienced many of what I like to term "aha moments", meaning moments when the light goes on in your head and you learn a good lesson about what makes you tick.

When you return home after a day's training, especially after you have learned something about yourself and your ability to perform that you didn't know before now, or that you forgot only to re-learn today, you need to put pen to paper. I will bet that it is not your tendency to write down your lessons learned – few are the athletes I've met who keep notes about the things they learn along the way. On the other hand, few are the athletes who really know themselves and what makes them tick in detail. Dare to be different from most and write down your training insights and keep a record of those insights.

Logbooks, believe it are not, will become the answer to your prayers – your best friend when it comes to training deliberately. When you return home from a day's training, a few times each week make some notes about the sorts of things you did that day – all day, leading up to, and then throughout your training session(s). Choose days when you had an exceptional or a sub-par performance, then back track and dissect the ingredients that produced the performance. Write up to 1-2 pages when analyzing the ingredients that led up to the performance, and consider the amount of sleep you had the night before, what and when you ate throughout the day, what your mood was, how you got along with others during the day, and then dissect your focus and the chronology of that focus as you went deeper into the day's training / learning session. In addition, on a given day where you learn something unique about yourself that you want to remember, write that insight down and place a star beside the insight.

At the end of each month you have a task to do that will put closure on the month's deliberate training. Go through the month's notes, which should amount to about 8-9 training entries and maybe a few one-sentence additions on days where you gained an insight about yourself. As you read through the month's notes, have two highlighters close by. One highlighter should be used to identify insights of things you would like to integrate every day in training as part of a systematic approach to training. The second highlighter should be used for insights and items you have learned about yourself, that you wish not to repeat ongoing as part of your deliberate training. Then, create a section in the last page or two of your notebook that is devoted to summary facts – a sort of to do and not to do list. The back section I am talking about should be in two columns with the to do items in the first column and the not to do items in the second column. Eventually, what you will find is that you have a comprehensive approach to training that is summarized in a page or two – a sort of Coles Notes just about you and what you need to remember each day before you engage in deliberate training.

Review your notes at the start of each day and remember that learning things about yourself once is a very efficient and systematic way to progress toward boxing excellence. Each time you make mistake is a great opportunity to learn, but committing the very same mistake several times in a row, or also over years of training, makes for inefficient learning.

FINAL REFLECTIONS

In this chapter we tackled the subject of deliberate training. There is a pile of information out there about the subject, simply go on the web and search for "deliberate practice". If you go to the very essence of what we've discussed in this chapter, your focus needs to be on mindful training, meaning that you need to make decisions before, during, and after training that bring you closer to systematic improvement. There are many insights you can gain from yourself when you engage in deliberate training. Some of those insights might be about remembering to stay true to your goals and making decisions each day that bring you closer to those goals. Another lesson could relate to the structure you take from before you walk into the gym through to the moments you walk out of the gym and beyond!

There are lots of crumbs to pick up, meaning details that you need to think about in relation to your training, and how to maximize that training. Each day provides an opportunity to bank a few more hours of attention to details. Over time, your banked hours will help you materialize into the level of boxer that stands above the others around you. There is a saying that "the devil is in the details". I agree with that saying, and hopefully, so do you after reading this chapter. There is no time like the present to become a details oriented boxer. After all you are a boutique operation, and your abilities need to be built from a firm foundation of focused training and know how.

When athletes bank the lesson they need to learn through deliberate training, they become the sorts of boxers who under pressure resort to the correct decisions. Great decisions under pressure don't just happen, even though many believe that they do just materialize. Good habits are the result of many invested hours in good decision, hours that are banked in the gym. Commit to deliberate training today and stay committed to that process over time. If you do what I propose, the dividends are yours to harvest, and you can bet that in those crucial moments in the ring, they will be there for you to resource when you need them most.

Chapter 6

WORKING IN HARMONY WITH COACHES AND OTHERS IN THE GYM

For years now, one of my most important roles is that of creating team harmony among athletes, coaches, and sport science providers. If someone were to ask me, and many have, why my athletes progress very quickly to their global boxing status in the professional ranks, I always explain the importance of an integrated team. The best athlete, with the best coach, and the best sport science providers, still can fall short in performance when resources are not coordinated effectively through communicating. If people have knowledge, and that knowledge is either not shared, or shared and not heard, those resources are wasted. As you will correctly guess, there is nothing worse than inefficient learning, and some of what determines efficiency from inefficiency in a boxer's development pertains to team harmony.

I have worked in many national team and professional boxer training camps over almost the last twenty years of my life. Though there is such a thing as "puncher's luck", other than that, I can usually predict whether my client will best or be bested by his opponent, dependent on how my client's team functions. When that team pulls together, it is easy to overcome even the most challenging of opponents, including opponents who are on pound for pound listings – no problem. On the other hand, if the team doesn't gel, meaning that we don't all pull in the same direction, the challenge posed by our next opponent looms much larger. Wins and losses are foreseeable – all one needs to do is look at how the athlete's team functions.

Not long ago, I worked with a client who was deliberating whether to accept the opportunity of a world title bout. The athlete he would have to fight was (and still is) a big puncher – that opponent is dangerous. When the athlete and his management team sat around the table going back and forth on whether to accept the fight, all of the boxer's team were convinced that the opportunity was an opportunity of a life time. We believed that with the correct preparation and a complete focus, our boxer could pull out a win, and so dethrone the world champion. But, we also looked deeper and compared our team with the team the opponent was surrounded by. Our team was comprised of a coach who was (and continues to be) a student of the sport, even as his athletes are among the world's best, we had a technical coach with a doctorate, who also produced more than twenty Olympic Gold Medalists, and I also brought a doctorate and more than fifteen years producing world champions to the table. In addition, our cut man was also a world champion coach, successful sports commentator, and a highly intelligent businessman. Our team also, is comprised of people who are also good friends. When we are in the same city together, we typically go for lunch, discuss boxing, work out differences, and essentially, continue to develop.

Across the ring was a formidable athlete, also with some very good resources. However, his team was not as formidable as ours, and I knew that the contrast of the two teams would make a formidable difference by fight night. The opponent was a great athlete, with a strong amateur pedigree. His corner was also comprised of a working team who produced previous world champions, including the client himself. However, the opposing team was not a well-gelled team. The athlete lacked trust in his management group, and we knew that. All we needed to do was be ourselves and the insecurity of the opponent would eventually surface – and it did. By the time fight night came, our athlete was the aggressor and the champion was much more cautious. Athletes gain their strength not only from their internal resources. They also gain confidence by who they surround themselves with, and how those resources work in collaboration.

In this chapter I am going to share with you some of my philosophy of what a team needs to look like. You might not have the sort of team I am laying out for you, at least not right now. However, teams are built from people, and people can either pull together or fall apart. There is an old saying that Jesse James, a world-renowned stagecoach robber shared with his team when he felt that they needed to pull together. He said the following "Either we hang together or we hang alone". What follows are suggestions of how to pull your team together.

SELECTING TEAM MEMBERS

There are lots of ways to define "the best" people to build your team with. Not long ago, the US Basketball Team played in the 2004 Olympics. They have always referred to themselves as "The Dream Team". On paper, the United States should have an obvious edge over all other countries when it comes to Olympic Basketball because that country is well-stocked with great athletes. Look no further than the number of NBA basketball players and surely a Dream Team can be selected. However, even in that sport it was realized after a devastating loss at the Olympics that great on paper and great in reality can be two very different discussions.

In boxing, amateur and professional, I have watched boxers move from coach to coach in search of the right fit. Such athletes tend to go with big name coaches, who are great on paper, but are sometimes also tight for time, over-committed, and in a few instances, over-rated. Such athletes generally tend to go with what they see on paper, and don't look beneath the surface at what is really inside the package and the wrapping. There needs to be much more than a great paper record for each and every member of your working team. There must also be "chemistry". Either that chemistry is there, or it isn't. When team members have chemistry, both with you, the boxer, and also among themselves, the team's pieces fit together much like a puzzle that comes together into a wonderful and vivid picture. On the other hand, when even the most well-known working staff member doesn't fit within the team, it is sometimes much the same as trying to fit a square peg into a round hole.

One professional boxer in particular comes to mind when I think of someone whose team has not come together well. Though I cannot give you the particulars of the case, the boxer is a great boxer, and he also has a fantastic coach and a well-known promoter. The promoter (who will remain nameless) has thrown his boxer under the bus, so to speak by criticizing the boxer's performance, even after a win. Over time the boxer and promoter have been at odds and the cost has been to the boxer's performance in the ring. A boxer who is quite frankly extremely good has been cut down smaller than his size due to the incorrect selection of a promoter.

People in a team have to really like each other. Some might say that business is business, and that it is unimportant for members to really be friends outside the ring. However, what sort of staff would you go the distance for – the distant one or the one that has invested emotionally into you? Recently, there was a double feature on HBO, where Derek Alexander was the main feature. If you look to Derek and his coach, and I cannot comment on the particulars, you see a coach and athlete who are very committed to each other. You also need that kind of commitment to the people you choose, and the people you choose must also have the very same commitment to you! Look beneath the numbers at the very essence of the people you are surrounding yourself with. If you have a great feeling about those people, you are well on your way to greatness. Daily training is challenging enough, the people you surround yourself with need to be a source of inspiration to counter such challenges.

Laying the Ground Work through Communication

So where does good communication begin? It begins with you! Recently I watched a young prospect box in his professional debut, and within the athlete's professional name, was a word that suggested he would be quiet and silent in all things related to his emerging career. I guess some people believe that speaking is done in the ring, which is true for the most part. I am not a big fan of boxers who talk far too much, and in fact, talk their way into extensive pressure, and downward performance. However, when it comes to working in your team, you cannot be silent. I know the athlete just mentioned as I met him when the athlete was an amateur. That athlete was silent with just about everyone, including those who were trying to prepare him for challenging amateur bouts. Silence such as his is not the answer to a successful progression and evolution in boxing.

Boxers and those around them need to be transparent with the people who are positioned to help them within the working team. Differences in opinion and views around almost anything, from choices in opponent, to the selection of types of gloves, to how a corner should work to bring out the best in you, all needs to be discussed openly. Words should never remain unspoken, because when they do, the people around us can only guess at what we are thinking, what we need, what works well, and what needs to be re-visited and modified in that boutique approach that you need. Guess work is an imperfect system. The better way to approach things is for you to exchange ideas and views with those who work with you, and also, ask them to take the very same approach as they work with you!

I have worked with many a coach and athlete who lack in communication transparency. Those sorts of people often find themselves disappointed by the people they work with. People are not mind readers, and even the most astute and sensitive of people cannot always read what is on your mind, and therefore, what you need. The very same point applies to coaches and for that matter, anyone else you might be working with, now and in the future. The important thing to always remember must be open lines of communication, even on basic things. You and those you work with need to develop the habit of good communication each day so that when that communication matters most, meaning when you are under pressure, good communication will be maintained. Good communication needs to be practiced and perfected. Remember that most people are not by nature great communicators. You need to work on open lines of communication every day. I will say this: of all the elite amateur and professional athletes I have worked with, the ones who became the most successful over time were great communicators. Success is built in part on trusting that your communication will be heard, respected, and then considered in a meaningful way. If you wish for that level of listening by those around, you must first listen to them, and really look to understand their perspectives.

So, start today and see if you can communicate better in training. If you don't fully understand something, try not to do what most people would do, meaning nod their heads as if they understand. Instead, ask for clarification and really try to get at what your coach is saying, and then integrate what you have just heard. By doing so, you can start on a process of listening to those around you. From there, if you become a good listener, and others feel heard, they will in turn listen more carefully to what you are saying. To often we go through our lives busy, moving from task to task without prioritizing communication. The thing you need to remember is that we live in a world of people, and to really progress well, we need to always progress from good to better communication, each day.

DEVELOPING BOUNDARIES FOR EACH MEMBER'S CONTRIBUTION

As you go deeper into your evolution as a boxer, you might find that you have added additional members to your team. I have found that as team's evolve and also, expand in number, the maintenance of interpersonal relationships becomes that much more important. Recently, I have worked with a professional boxer with an extensive support team, comprised of coaching staff, sport science staff, medical staff, and managerial staff. At times I have found that the different groupings of staff within his team are entirely unaware of what other members contribute. In the past I was once told by an experienced professional coach that he did not want to know the functions of the other members in his team. The athlete was a world champion, and yet the components of his team did not connect with one another. The left hand seemed not to know what the right hand was doing.

When athletes and coaches step into the ring for competition they need to understand that they are stepping into performance based on a foundation of knowledge, built from the contributions of team members. The pieces of the athlete's preparation have to fit together and the only way to know that they really do is by understanding the contributions of each respective member. Far too often, when athletes step into the ring, they just assume that their team are doing a fantastic job and that there is no need to really understand the complexity, meaning how the unique parts of preparation piece together into a working system. Though athletes need to simplify their lives, meaning you also, to do so you need to really understand that the basis are being covered.

Coaches and working teams often do a great job, and sometimes they don't even really take the time to understand why their team is working as well as it is. By understanding what each member does, you could look at how team members contribute to you, and really get to the bottom of how well prepared you really are. Sometimes there are overlaps in the work of a few team members, so in those cases, understanding each person's contributions allows you to simplify your team by either assigning a specific role to only one member, or by having two members work together, collectively.

I guess you are getting the idea how important collaboration and the clarity of members' roles is to me, and also, to you. Let's consider the opposite scenario when people don't really understand how their contributions fit within your development. What happens in those cases begins with people overstepping their roles, and then, stepping onto the toes of another team member's responsibilities and specialization. Sometimes, overstepping happens quite by accident, and for a little while, nothing is said by the team member who is stepped on. For a while, you as an athlete might not notice that there are problems within your team, that is until there is a blow-up between two members. That blow-up will likely happen when you need a tight team the most, or just after a setback in your performance. By then, the opportunity to correct your team's roles is done reactively, and not, proactively.

When you develop boundaries for each member's contributions, you actively go about developing a very strong working team. As I said before, the right hand and the left hand really do need to understand what the other hand is doing. After all, in many cases, tasks only require hand, and not two! Now let's move forward in time to the last few minutes before an important bout, just as you are finishing your pre-bout warm-up, getting ready to step into the ring, and also when you are clearing your mind in the last few seconds before the bell that starts round one begins. In those critical seconds, you need to be clear of distractions, and you also need to know that your preparation was systematic and well integrated. Recently I witnessed a boxer on the Ring Magazine's Pound for Pound list fall apart just before a bout because he did not have faith in at least the contributions of one team member surrounding him. The pieces of every boxer's team must bind together, they must be supportive, and their contributions must be clear, concise, and positive.

THE PROGRESSIVE TEAM

Teams in harmony need to continue their development, even when they are at the top of their game. Some years ago, I worked with a world champion who already defended his title several times. The team he was surrounded by, me included, were all well-qualified, capable individuals. However, at a specific moment in time we became complacent and we coasted on the athlete's success. I noticed things going wrong with the athlete, as did others on his team, and we said nothing. We figured the athlete would get through his next fight and then maybe, we could tighten things up a little. Before we knew it, the fight was upon us and the athlete, much like his team, was coasting into the fight. You can guess what happened on fight night. My client lost his world title in a very close bout, one that he could have easily won had we all pulled together.

Teams need to be built with people committed to ongoing learning and also, an edgy philosophy, where the past success is looked upon as a stepping-stone to advancement. The question must always be "where do we go from here", and not only "look at the amazing things that we have already accomplished". Satisfaction with past success alone often leads to laziness and a lack of exploration into the sorts of details that made for a great preparation.

Success is found in the crumbs and the details, not only in the big picture. The progressive team needs to continue to ask themselves where details can be found to improve performance. The boxer needs to be at the center of that discussion, pushing his/her team to ongoing growth and development. Even in success there are lessons to be found and then integrated.

Though we will look very closely at some of the ways to identify those details in Chapter Fifteen when we discuss post-bout debriefings, the detailed approach you and your team need to take must be taken, daily. Laziness comes before the fall. When people rest on their laurels they are dethroned by a more progressive boxer, surrounded by a very progressive team. So how might you and your team engage in a progressive approach where you are all advancing at the same rate of growth? As I spelled out to you in Chapter Two, reading and watching video footage of well- and not-so-well managed teams can be useful educational resources. In addition, there is no substitute for team meetings. Just last week I sat in a three-hour team meeting with an extremely progressive athlete and working. The discussion was not on how our accomplished client could retain his title, but rather on what our concerns are regarding the next opponent. The concern was brought forward by our cutman and in that moment, he was reminding the team that we need to continue on our progressive path toward ongoing success. Without such meetings, where people are brought together, there cannot be the sort of honest discussion we engaged in.

My view is that far too often, working teams and the athletes they are built around do not adequately share and coordinate information effectively. There need to be opportunities for service providers to share information with each other, so that the members work in a coordinated effort toward the target of success. The bull's eye, so to speak, is progression, and progression can only happen when the left hand knows what the right hand is doing, and when the athlete understands how the pieces of his team fit together.

WORKING THROUGH DIFFERENCES

I have never met an athlete who hasn't experienced a difference of opinion with members of his/her working team. Within even the very best top-level teams, people have differences, and those differences serve as an opportunity to build an even better team. I suppose the first thing you need to accept is that no team is immune to differences in opinion, and the arguments that might result from such differences. I have learned over time that with differences comes the expansion of ideas, creative brainstorming, and better solutions, though only when space is made for a diversity of opinions. Remember at all times, differences in opinion are healthy: if you start with such an approach people will always share their opinions and potential mistakes in your preparation can be solved quickly and competently.

Working through differences is not ever easy. People always bring their own position to the table when discussing differences in perspective or approach. You and I, for example, likely share certain views in common, but we will also differ in our views on several things, also. When people hold differences in opinion, some try to bring the other person over to their perspective, so that only one person is being asked to adjust, or change. If you believe that in negotiations there is always a winner and a loser, then you likely go about having other people adapt and modify their perspective so that it matches with yours. When person becomes the loser in the discussion, he/she will quickly lose ownership over the discussion, and the emotional investment that comes along with it. When only some of the team is invested in a decision, the problem is that the rest of the team doesn't really buy into the direction that needs to be taken for you to progress onward to your potential.

There are other people who believe that if they are asked to shift in their position, that no one else should get what they want, also. Recently, I have heard stories about a boxer who is presently in training camp. The boxer is miserable because he is being asked to train away from his home city and devote his focus entirely to boxing for six weeks. The boxer's staff is committed to the athlete sticking it out and preparing for the full six weeks in advance of an important televised fight. The athlete views the strong stance of his support team, and their insistence in him staying put as the team forcing him. The boxer's team is clearly the winners as seen through the athlete's eyes, and the athlete then sees himself as defeated and disempowered. Thought the athlete will persist in the training camp, the outcome within that one decision has now trickled into many other aspects of the boxer's preparation. He has now decreased his effort and enthusiasm within the training camp, and it seems that even his onsite coaching staff are having a miserable time with him, so much so that the coach is looking to find new lodgings, where the environment is more positive – meaning away from the athlete. Within the story just described, the loss to the athlete is now becoming loss also, to the athlete's coaching and managerial staff – all people involved are miserable.

What I am trying to push you toward is discussions that are winners for all people around the table. We must always be willing to change a personal position, if there is the opportunity to make a better collaborative decision, where you as athlete benefit most. Coaches and team members need to first commit to listening to the diversity of opinions around the table and consider each opinion in terms of its merit before dismissing anyone's opinion out of hand. It is easy to make a snap decision and stick to one's own position, at least in the short-term! In the long-term it is far better to listen to the diversity of opinions around the table and then arrive at a collaborative approach where the right hand and the left hand work together to push through challenges. Recently, a professional boxer was in earshot of his working team, while we worked through differences in opinion regarding how to present information to that athlete. At the end of a heated discussion among his team, the athlete asked me what all of the arguing about. In fact, the coaching staff members sitting around the table that memorable evening continue to agree that the meeting was among the best they have encountered to that point in our collective careers as staff to many world champions. The athlete quickly came to realize that disagreement and heated discussion, is sometimes very productive. The outcome of that discussion early in the athlete's training camp ended in the athlete winning a Ring Belt and unified world professional championship.

NEW ADDITIONS TO THE WORKING TEAM

Teams tend to be a little dynamic over time, though hopefully not too dynamic. I know of several high profile amateur and professional boxers who've changed their team members, meaning those who coach and provide services, many times over the course of a career. The goal of boxers needs to be geared toward progression, though also continuity, where the past links correctly with the present and the future. Every boxer comes with a past, and I have noticed that many times, when boxers engage in frequent changes in their support team, their performances decline.

Teams need continuity so that each member knows where she/he fits within the larger group, as I have outlined earlier in this chapter. Every member must belong and have a distinct role within your development, as a contributing team member. With a well-oiled team, each member gets to know who you are as a boxer and really, what makes you tick. That sort of understanding is not something to be rushed – it takes lots of time to learn how any boxer works at best. When athletes change their team composition, they might gain some better-qualified member, but often, it will take the new member some time to come up to speed.

Far too often, boxers make changes in their team's composition in search of an answer that they believe will be found in a new addition to the team. Little do such boxers know that many of the answers they are looking for are already available, providing the boxer looks inward and really considers what he needs in order to be at his best. So, I am not a big supporter of ongoing change within any boxer's team composition. Even when I start working with a new client, though I know my area of expertise, how I approach the athlete is guess work until I really work with that athlete, listen to him/her, and then consider what the athlete wants in relation to a few pressure-filled performances. Recently I was added to an athlete's team just before he fought for an interim professional world title. I have known the coach and the athlete for many years, but I did not worked with that athlete for several years until re-engaging with him a few months ago. I think we worked well together, as does he and his coach. However, there were aspects that I really did not know about the athlete, including what his optimal level of arousal should be before he enters the ring. Every athlete is different, and it takes team members a while to really get to know the athletes they work with.

Even with the athlete discussed directly above, there needed to be a starting point in terms of his motivational program, and so we started work with the athlete on his mental game. New members inevitably will join your support team from time to time, though hopefully those new additions will not change regularly, as you need to be surrounded with people who know your past, present, and future, not just those who promise you a future, without a full understanding of your history, patterns, preferences, and tendencies.

When new members join the team, they need to fit into the larger team and also provide their technical expertise. So, new additions need to blend into the group on two levels, and not just based on their experience / expertise. Team members must know their area and how to help you, but first, they must blend well into the team. Team harmony is huge – without you could have the best service providers, though each member will not connect to the other members in a synergistic way. A member of my working team always shares a philosophy that we all share, at the very beginning of each training camp, just as we are starting work with a high profile client in advance of his next well-televised bout. He says the words "team is team". Meaning that team is everything, with it an athlete can reach unanticipated heights and win over much more experienced opponents, just by pulling together. New members in a team must also hang together as part of the team, and they must belong and be trusted by you the client, but also by other members within the team.

I have known over the last fifteen years many team members with all of the credentials in the world, who even with those credentials, took away more than they added to the team's synergy. There is nothing wrong with building a comprehensive team, providing that team is carefully chosen, not only based on technical qualifications, but also based on their personality and capacity to belong as a team member.

FINAL REFLECTIONS

On occasion you will find a sport psychology handbook where team harmony is discussed. Even with sport researchers affirming the importance of team harmony, many boxers overlook its importance when selecting and modifying their teams. There is much more to the word "team" than meets the eye. You can have the greatest team on paper, and the team might not really gel into a well-oiled unified group. When the group is comprised only of people with individual agendas, the single and shared goal of excellence in the ring will be lost.

Good teams are entitled to their differences, and even their disagreements. There is nothing wrong, and in fact everything right about hashing out differences. Teams are built from several individuals, and each person, including you, will have a unique perspective to bring to the table. With several different views of how to work through a challenge or a difference of opinion, unique ideas will be generated. Not everyone will agree on a given idea and which of the many ideas brought to the table should be used. Because people have differences, those differences need to be put on the table for all of the membership to consider and discuss. From openness amongst team members, creative solutions happen, hopefully bringing together several views into a better solution than can be created by any individual.

Good teams are also progressive teams, meaning that teams must continue to learn from each other. Even after an excellent performance, the team must consider past choices, re-use what has worked in the past, and also add to it so that you continue to move forward, no matter how successful you are. The worst thing that can happen is when teams sleep after a notable success, and they become comfortable, and in fact lazy, in what they do. Good teams are not sleeping teams. Great teams are highly energetic, always on the move, and learning new things to share with the other members. You, the athlete, must always feel that you are progressing forward to a higher level of achievement, and the team you surround yourself with must support your advancement.

Chapter 7

BEING POSITIVE MINDED AND PERSISTENT

Some years ago I witnessed a coach working the corner of an amateur athlete at a national championship. The coach was trying to be positive, and in a desperate minute in between the third and fourth round he exclaimed "come on, be positive". The athlete looked at him with vacant eyes, not knowing how to connect his coach's message with the final few minutes of performance that were directly in front of him.

Athletes do need to be positive, boxers included. But, there is much more to being positive than just the outcome of being happy or being aggressive, or otherwise. Based on forty years of advanced research in motivational psychology we now know exactly what the formula is to creating the agenda that the coach above hoped for in the final moments of his boxer's performance. Positive-mindedness is a habit, and even though the coach did not realize it, it is a habit that results from focused work that begins in the gym and transplants into performance in the ring.

In this chapter, we are going to take the time and clarify for you how to create a positive mindset. Also, being positive is important, but not adequate if you are looking for the ongoing solution-oriented focus needed to really bring your game to the next level. As you will see, there is much more than meets the eye when it comes to developing a positive focus. Positive focus doesn't just happen, you need to think and speak to yourself and others in a way that confirms your positive focus. What you think and what you say will become what you do. First, let's look at the puzzle pieces that are the foundation to positive and a negative focus.

THE LANGUAGE OF POSITIVE MINDEDNESS

Everything we think, we think through words and feelings. The words that we use are more than just meaningless expressions, even though most of us go through our day without much thought in terms of the influence of what we say on what we do. Every word that leaves your mouth, or the mouth of a team member, can have value, either positive or negative. Have you ever noticed a teammate who enters into the gym and always brings down the collective energy of others around him/her? What really happens when that person enters the gym? Let me describe one possible scenario: Your teammate enters the gym with a low level of energy, complains about being tired, and expresses that he isn't looking forward to today's training.

When the athlete above starts speaking, what is the first thing that enters your mind? Do you feel energized or somewhat de-energized? It's easy to spot in a teammate when he/she is down in energy. I wonder how often such athletes ever go about pulling up their bootstraps and self-energizing through a change in word choices? From the athletes I have witnessed, even for those who do not share their thoughts with those around them, when a person is down, they always tend to use self-talk, meaning internal thinking and speaking, to confirm their negative thoughts.

The value of word choices when you go through the day is profound. The words you choose influence whether you feel good or bad, whether you are angry, sad, happy, and even persistent. So, you need to start keeping track of what you say, both to yourself and to those around you. Every word that leaves your mouth or bounces around in your thinking can make a difference in terms of the value of a day's training. As we discussed several chapters ago, a day's training is an investment, with a good day's training adding one more penny into your developmental piggybank. There is no telling which day's investment will make the difference between greatness and goodness. For any day to be a great day, you need to walk the walk and carry into that day, a certain swagger, and also, a certain language.

Given that words are valuable, you need to choose the right words each day. Sentences that start with "I will" or "I can" help you engage in solution-oriented thinking. Every word you choose needs to help you move toward imposing control over today's training, meaning every piece of today's training from dressing, to skipping rope, onward to shadow boxing, and through the day's training plan. BY choosing words that push you to engage and self-energize you are investing in a better day's training, and also, a habit that you need to employ tomorrow, and also, during the days that follow tomorrow.

If you notice that you are talking yourself out of energy and the commitment to today's training, correct your language – do something about what you say. You do not need to be a passive bystander to your own self-talk. You need to craft your self-talk so that you mean business when you engage in every minute of training. If someone around you is using words that take away from the energy that you are trying to build, I suppose you must make the decision to either help that person to re-energize, or you must focus inward to what you can control, meaning your own use of words.

WHERE WE LEARN OUR LANGUAGE

Some years ago, I completed my doctorate. As a topic for my research, I chose to look at Canadian Olympians in order to understand why some excel under pressure where others seem to wilt and under-achieve. Though the details of the project are not all that essential to our discussion here, one little lesson does hold some value. Every positive-minded athlete seemed to learn her/his word choices by the people in his coaching and sport science team. Especially head coaches seemed to be influential to the way the athletes thought and expressed themselves as potential successful or unsuccessful competitors. When the head coach was positive about the athlete's abilities, the athlete learned to evaluate his capacities in the very same way! When coaches referred to their athletes as "persistent" and "blue-collar" in their work ethic, their athletes learned to judge themselves as hard workers, but not necessarily as talented performers.

Going a step further, the way coaches viewed judges also contributed to what athletes learned to view their chances of success. I recall one particular well-known coach from elite amateur and professional boxing, who viewed all judges as biased and unpredictable. When I worked with the coach's athletes, all were skeptical about their chances of success given the supposed unpredictability of their judges. So, what the coach shared with his athletes, became their frame of reference, and in this case, their diminished chance of success. I have noticed when considering the career of that coach, all of his athletes eventually moved to other coaches, in search of a more positive approach to boxing performance. To this day, the aforementioned coach does not understand why his athletes eventually move elsewhere – that reason being how he presents boxing challenges to his boxers. Every boxer is always looking for that positive approach, and the approach must come from within, but also from the coach the boxer trains with, and learns from.

The way boxers view themselves might also come from other sources of support, such as family members, partners, teammates, and even friends. If you hang out with a group of people often enough, you will tend to adopt their expressions, their vocabulary, and even their emotional responses. Think about people who are positive or negative in terms of the energy they give off. When among positive charged people, we gain in energy. When around negative people, we tend to lose energy, slow our speech, and eventually, mirror back the very same negative emotions we are surrounded by. The objective, always, is to surround yourself with positive-minded, and therefore positive speaking support, and not those who present themselves as realists or pessimists.

Typically, coaches and athletes do not realize that they are using positive or negative language when it comes to their own likelihood of success or the chance of success of others they work or train with. If you were asked to consider whether you have a positive or negative outlook about your likelihood of success, that question could be easily answered. But, you might not realize the root cause for your more general tendency and outlook as a boxer. It might take someone pointing out to you your language use, and the words you choose to describe yourself and your situation. Talk and self-talk play a big part in your overall attitude toward training and performance, and so you need to "choose your words wisely", as the saying goes.

LOOKING BENEATH THE CURTAIN

So you might wonder now how to evaluate whether the words you choose add or take away from your development and your performance. Let me start off by sharing a story with you, one that was shared with me when I was a child:

> Two children were invited to participate in a psychological experiment. One child was placed in a room filled with toys, colorful slides, swings, and every tasty food that a child could ever dream of. The child was told that he has a full day to enjoy the room, and then he was left under observation.
>
> The second child (not literally) was placed in a horse barn that happened to be filled with three feet of horse manure, and only a pitchfork. This child, again was provided with a day's time and left to do whatever activities he saw fit to do.
>
> The day cam and went, and so the psychology researcher returned first to the child left earlier with all of the toys. When the psychologist arrived he noticed that the child sat in the corner of the room, that he had not touched any of the toys, and that despite all of the food

provided, all of it was left untouched. The child essentially was hungry. When asked why he had not engaged with the great objects left in his room, the child responded that he didn't want to break any of the toys, and also, he feared being injured. When asked why he hadn't touched the food, the response was that the child feared that he would get an upset stomach from all of the rich food.

Next, the psychology researcher returned to the horse barn. He was surprised to find that the child in the barn was in a sweat and that there was a large hole dug with the pitchfork, that went right down to the concrete, and so, through the manure. The psychologist looked on in amazement and asked the child what on earth he was doing. The child responded simply that with all of the horse manure, he was in the midst of searching for the pony that went with it.

Words and thoughts take us on journeys toward and away from effort. When the two children above were left in what should conventionally have inspired a certain action, both seemed to choose unlikely behaviors, based upon reasoning they had walking into their experiences. So, it is not necessarily the circumstance we face that results in a positive or a negative response. Instead, what determines our actions is how we evaluate the situation we are in, either with inspiring or uninspiring language and then, the thinking that follows our language choices.

The challenge we all face is how we choose to respond to the circumstances we face, be those circumstances training, competition, or the interpersonal relationships we need in both instances, in order to bring our best foot forward. There are opportunities in moment, providing we see them, pick up the pitchfork, and then get to work with enthusiasm. After all, it is not the opportunity you have in front of you, but your approach to that opportunity that will determine whether you progress as a boxer.

A STRUCTURE FOR PERSISTENCE

There are several ways to develop persistence through your use of self-talk and talk with others. The tricks of the trade vary depending on the circumstance obviously, though generally, there is an approach that you can use after a great performance, and another approach that can be used after a setback in performance. After a great performance, you need to explain that performance to strategies and decisions you and your team employed leading up to the performance. Great performances don't just happen. Some boxers believe that they have great performances that surfaced out of nowhere, unexplainably. The reality is that great performances happen for several reasons. When I work with my high profile clients, we always debrief after a performance, within the first 24 hours post-bout. The objective is for our team to start looking for the small – minute crumbs that in total, contributed to the great performance.

Underlying our discussion, the boxer needs to understand that a great performance is the result of lots of small decisions. As I have said all along, every boxer is a boutique operation, and the decisions made by and for the boxer need to match with who he/she is as an athlete. As we dissect the great performance, and all of the technical, tactical, and logistical things that amounted to the performance, I take very thorough notes to document what the athlete has learned. The goal is to learn from what works and then to integrate those lessons into the boxer's performance plan leading up to and then during the next bout. The details are then taken back to the boxer for feedback in the form of a written report.

Why the paperwork and the lengthy debriefing process that we will re-visit in much more detail during Chapter 15? Most boxers bask in their glory immediately after a fantastic bout, and do not take the time to really make sense of the causes that ended in a great performance. You want to be more than just confident; you want to be knowledgeable about what makes you tick. Through lots of discussion and exploration, the goal is for you to walk away from your performance knowing that what you need to do in order to control your performance, and so, make the right decisions during the next bout, also. Bottom line: you need to search for "controllable" factors.

Some boxers believe when they are on a roll that their success will continue permanently. I have worked with several athletes who believe after success, that the next bout will also end in success because they have a history of success. As you could well agree, some boxers do know what it takes to win. However, great performances are not a given. Even in wins, I have witnessed athletes who've walked away from such performances far less confident than they were before the bout. For those who walk away with a win, be that win facilitative of confidence or not, the reality is that there must always be a search for why the bout ended as it did. Success does not just happen, and we cannot just assume it will continue to happen. Even for the most formidable of boxers, success eventually is not a foregone conclusion. In fact, if you read Ring Magazine, there is a section devoted to "Sting Rays". The feature in the section is an athlete who out of nowhere, and with a lesser bout record, upsets a much more successful boxer. If we look beyond the person who pulled off the upset, and consider the person who was surprisingly defeated, we see someone who likely incorrectly anticipated his success, and then was caught out. Bottom line: success cannot be assumed.

It is far easier to evaluate setbacks. Every boxer searches for meaning after a loss. The important things when searching for meaning and making sense of that loss, are (1) to look for times and decisions where control was given up, and (2) to be as forgiving of others as typically you would be of yourself, while engaging in a more critical self-evaluation. Let's consider each one of the two points with a little more detail.

There tends to be a pattern in people not to really look closely at their setbacks, either because it is extremely hard one one's ego, or because the setback is assumed to be a temporary problem that will resolve itself. For some boxers it is really difficult to be hard on oneself, though far easier to be critical of the people who prepared you for the performance. In social psychology they call such a tendency a "fundamental attribution error". It is far easier to attack someone else, only because it deflects the negative emotions that follow after a setback. Where the boxer who looks inward might feel the emotions of shame or guilt, the boxer who deflects responsibility to a coach or official can feel anger, and also, no responsibility. The important thing to remember is that you need to take responsibility for your setbacks, just like you take responsibility after a great performance. If you place yourself as the place where the buck stops, then you can do what follows that sort of thinking and speaking – you can change things for the better.

Next, you do need to consider the role of your coaching staff and others who've also contributed to the performance. If you have witnessed a teammate assigning blame to a coach, you saw that beneath his anger there was the hidden (or maybe not so hidden) belief that the coach made the incorrect decision, intentionally. The people around you are also engaged in a learning process, and they too, will make mistakes that need to be modified as they progress in their role. You need to make space in your evaluations for your support staff to make and then correct their missteps. In addition though, you must first make certain that the mistakes assigned to others are actually their mistakes and not yours. Bottom line: accountability is very important, and at very least, some of the accountability belongs to you.

TESTING WORD CHOICES

There are two important things to do in order to test your word choices, meaning whether your words build or take away from your persistence. The first way is highly personal, and requires you to look closely at the sort of internal self-talk (word choices) you use before and during a day's training, and also before and during a bout. During times when you feel highly energetic, I want you to look inward and identify the words and thought that are coming to your mind. As I shared with you, though good things might come to your mind, the objective is to have them at the forefront of your mind often, not just on occasion.

The next step I am going to ask of you is a "big ask". I want you to take a few seconds at those critical times each day and write down the sorts of word choices you are making. Documenting your words in a sort of note pad, is a means of reinforcing good word choices. You will find after a month or so that certain word choices connect with really good thinking, and afterward, really good training and competition performance. I want you to know with certainty the sorts of words that push you in the correct direction so that you could use those very same words with consistency. I find that with boxers, just like most every other athlete, moods and energy levels seem to go up and down. What you need is an up mood as much of the time as you can secure it. Doing so will maximize your effort each day, to the point where you will make the necessary gains others don't benefit from. Title this section of your notebook "words I thought".

You need to also evaluate the words to choose when speaking with others, and the words others use when speaking with you. In terms of the words you use with others, meaning your coaches and teammates, those also need to be documented in a separate section titled "words shared". The words you put out there and share with other have a compounded influence on the approach you take to training and bout performance. First, the minute words leave your mouth, you actually hear them. In hearing the words you choose, you reinforce a certain way of thinking, in the very same way that you influence your thinking through self-talk. Unlike the old saying, "talk is not cheap", talk is loaded with value, though only sometimes is that value beneficial to you. Second, by sharing words with others, you also influence them and contribute to the mood in your training environment. Such words, by influencing those around you, come back to you in a boomerang-like way when others take on the thinking you have just shared through word choices. When your word choices are good, I like to term those choices a "double dividend". The words influence you both directly and indirectly. So, choose the words you share, wisely.

The people you train with or seek help from in the midst of bout performance also have thoughts and language of their own. The words they bring to the performance table are just as important as yours. When a training and performance environment is focused, constructive, and solution oriented, good performance tends to emerge. On the other hand, I have been witness to athletes surrounded by problem focused coaches and teammates. The progress for such athletes tends to be an up hill battle, given that the approach taken to boxing is negative and counter productive. One particular coach I observed in a national team training camp was always negative about international tournament experiences, and he would share his negativity in the weeks leading up to the tournament. By the time he and his athletes arrived at the competition venue, his athletes looked completely defeated, with shoulders slumped, and no visible signs of positive motivation. Words influence, and they also contaminate boxing environments. The question becomes what sort of contamination are we looking for, positive or negative? I look to support and sometimes help design environments where positive contamination happens. In those sorts of contexts, good performances always emerge.

Words such as "can", "will", and "great", connected with technical and tactical directives provide the sort of ambition and clear-minded thinking that boxers need to have. The constructive words that you eventually identify as part of your logbook need to be maintained over time. You need to keep a close eye on the words you think and also share, especially when you are tired. You can monitor your word choices personally, though you should also have your coach keep a close eye on the words you share with him/her – especially if you are a little weak in this area of language. In exchange, you could also provide some monitoring for your teammates, and in so doing, improve the overall performance environment you are developing in.

FINAL REFLECTIONS

As we close down Chapter Seven, I hope you are walking away from this chapter with a strong awareness of just how important language choices, meaning the words you think and speak, are to your boxing performance. As I have said all along to this point in the book, there are many talented athletes who become blocked by weaknesses in their mental game. Some of those weaknesses originate in words and if you look through the newspaper and you tube interviews that even some of the most formidable boxers provide, when they stall out it seems that their way of describing their decline in performance matches with some of the language errors we have spoken about in this chapter.

Great boxers need to be great thinkers and great speakers. I recently sat and listened to Bernard Hopkins sharing his philosophy of boxing and why he achieved legendary status. He seems to choose his words wisely, more wisely in fact than most of his opponents. The self-belief and self-awareness that Hopkins has is not unique to Hopkins. It is simply that BHop has perfected his language over time, especially when we consider his earlier interviews with those he has provided over the last 4-5 years. Just as words have benefited Hopkins and also athletes like Muhammad Ali, so too can they benefit you. There is a lot to learn about the master craft of using your language to enhance your performance. Interestingly, boxers always marvel at the most self-assured of high profile athletes. Yet, few try to emulate the very same word choices in relation to their own performance. You need to be different; different is good.

My parting word to you on the subject of language is that you are what you say. Choose your words wisely and developing a performance environment where those around you buy into the very same philosophy. If you do so, you will be much more likely to stay on track with your thinking, and so, your doing.

SECTION TWO: BOUT PREPARATION

Chapter 8

ADAPTATION AND CONTINGENCY PLANS

There is always lots of talk among coaches about why athletes succeed and sometimes also fall short in their performances. Terms like "backyard performer" are voiced by many coaches as they seek to understand why their talented athletes don't deliver in the ring. In contrast, even among accomplished boxers, some athletes seem to deliver consistently despite tremendous odds. For example, some athletes travel and perform in foreign environments better than do others. Guys like Glen Johnson, the "Road Warrior", are known to perform as well on the road as they do at home. Other athletes found in the ShowTime's Super Six Tournament strongly believe that they need to be at home in order to win fights, and then advance deeper into that tournament. Each and every example that I have just raised for you speaks to a topic that I like to label as "athlete adaptation". Why adaptation: because an athlete's capacity to respond with flexibility and good decision-making is essential, especially in the most challenging of circumstances.

Each and every sport performance brings with it many challenges that you will need to act and react to in an effective way. Some athletes try to tackle challenges as they arise and then solve them on the fly, meaning in the moment. Others collaborate with their working teams and try to anticipate what some of the potential barriers to optimal performance might be, coming down the pike. Both types of athletes are looking to succeed in the ring, and in fact, both athletes hold the possibility of performing well dependent on their capacity to adapt.

There is no single way to adapt to the challenges you will encounter as a boxer. However, what I do know with certainty is that every great athlete must have a series of strategies that he uses to adapt and succeed in and out of the ring. Though such strategies are uniquely his / her own, there are certain guiding principles that inform better decisions over worse. Further, you might be surprised to know that adaptation is an ongoing objective that you will need to be mindful of each time you enter into a circumstance that is out of the ordinary and therefore, in need of your attention. What follows is a thorough discussion of adaptation, starting with a framework that you can use in the development of your own strategy.

DEFINING ADAPTATION

Over the course of the last five or so years, I have worked with sport researchers and applied sport psychologists from across the world, developing a workable set of skills that athletes and their coaches could use to respond at their best in stressful and challenging circumstances such as Olympics, world title bouts, etc. The basis of the work has been in relation to circumstances that often have overwhelmed even the best of athletes in the past. Though lots of boxers have the opportunities to fight at high profile tournaments such as the Ringside Tournament, on national teams, and also at the professional level, few have a well-developed understanding of how to adapt when they encounter a significant moment. Then again, few are the boxers who make it to the top and then hold a long reign as king of the division. The first rule of thumb is that athletes only need to adapt in situations that are unfamiliar, either in terms of the sport environment or the level of performance required.

As a boxer you will be very different in how much stress you can withstand leading up to and also during a performance. Some boxers can withstand lots of little stressors before they become anxious. Others are a little higher strung and it only takes a few stressors to push them to the point of being anxious. What all boxers hold in common is that at a certain point, they can become over-whelmed by the weight of the stressors they are experiencing in relation to a circumstance, such as an amateur tournament or a scheduled professional bout. In many cases, the piling up of stress happens over time, little by little. On occasion, the stressors might accumulate by the athlete over a much tighter period of time. Regardless, what separates the athlete who excels in performance from the one who goes downward in performance is his / her education and built from that education, the skills to make the right decisions in the moment. And so, adaptation is a positive response made by the boxer during the span of time when an unfamiliar circumstance is being experienced.

The athlete who adapts then, acts on his challenge, feels in control of the circumstances, and then approaches those circumstances with vigor. The end result for the adapted athlete is peak performance and accumulated confidence. Conversely, the athlete who is unable to adapt continues on the path to performance, though without the necessary skills to take control of himself before and during the performance. The consequence for the mal-adapted athlete is a decrease in confidence, less conviction, and a performance that is below potential. To me, there is no such thing as a backyard performer or a gym performer. Instead, those terms are just labels that we all assign to athletes who've never developed the correct adaptation skills, for moments when they need those skills most.

THE PATHWAYS TO ADAPTATION

If we stop to think about it, in the last few pages, we have started discussing how you can build adaptation skills. From studies I have co-authored about National Hockey League players, Canadian Olympians, Division One varsity team athletes, and also athletes from minority cultures, there are consistent pathways that can increase your capacity to act and react at your best before and during significant sport moments. The pathways are (1) understanding, (2) controlling, (3) self-enhancement, (4) trusting, and (5) belonging. I have found that any one of these pathways is a very good starting point to an adaptation strategy.

Also, in relation to each circumstance before you, one of the pathways will be more meaningful that the others. Start with one of the pathways below, though over time, my suggestion is that you develop several of the pathways for a more comprehensive approach to adaptation. A paragraph below will be devoted to each one of these pathways.

Understanding

I am a big advocate of athlete education. You might have a formal education, right through to the university level, and then again, you might not. Formal education is not the sort of education I am referring to here. Rather, when I support athletes in conjunction with my working team, the working team all understand that every athlete must understand what he is doing, and also why he is doing it! Some coaches are under the misconception that athletes follow rules – not us. If you really want to have a belief in yourself, meaning the sort of belief you will need to stand on during significant sport tests, you need to understand "the why" behind your training and competition techniques and tactics.

Earlier, I spoke about the importance of asking lots of question – see Chapter Two. There are lots of things you need to really understand on a deep level, if you want to succeed as a boxer. Some of the pieces to your education will pertain to understanding yourself. Self-aware athletes, first document (through a logbook) their training and performance activities, all the while looking for trends when they excel and also when they fall short. Though every athlete intuitively knows lots of what makes them tick, few have really researched themselves and arrived at their answers based on the systematic investigation that I encourage my athletes to engage in. Self-awareness is built on facts, and those facts are necessary in significant moments, when evidence is really what we need to rely on.

As you train in relation to a specific opponent, understanding also extends to understanding your opponent. I have spent much of my time the last 10 years working with professional boxers and their working teams. Initially, I believed that it was adequate to simply review videos of the opponent and while watching the video, look for his styles and tactics in performance. The last four years I have gone much deeper into the analysis of who my client's opponent is. I learn everything I can about the opponent, built from information easily gathered from the world-wide web. My professional boxing clients need to know what sorts of tactics their opponents will be up to through the media, in press conferences, during weigh-ins, when they step into the ring, and so on. By the time my client steps into the ring, very little can surprise him. As a result, my athletes are not over-loaded by what is coming at them from the opponent and his working team. And so, you need to understand yourself, but remember, in boxing, you do not perform in isolation – you need to understand the opponent also.

Finally, you need to understand the physical performance environment. At the beginning of this chapter I spoke about the ShowTime Super Six Tournament and how several of the competitors are under the misguided belief that hometown advantage in and of itself determines the outcome of each contestant. Having observed three bouts for each of the contestants, excluding those who withdrew, it seems as if for the most part, the athletes seem to exert more effort when on home ground. Because the athletes seem to buy into the concept of hometown advantage, most have decreased their efforts when traveling out of country to compete against their opponents. The interesting thing about the tournament is that the boxers have created a self-fulfilling prophecy. The final result from the Super Six Tournament will not be known to us, even by the time this book is published. However, it is extremely logical that sooner or later one of the contestants is going to have to win on the road. To do that, he will need to understand the environment where he will need to excel, in advance of his performance.

Understanding the performance environment might include an investigation into a suitable hotel, the appropriate training location for the final week before the fight, where to eat in advance of the fight, what the dressing room will look like in terms of size and privacy, and also what the stadium will be like on the night of performance. I recall working with one professional world champion who went to see a concert in the stadium he was readying to perform in, three days after the concert. Doing so got the athlete thinking about the size of the crowd and what the atmosphere would be like on fight night – at least to some extent.

Purring yourself at ease through the sorts of understanding I have just proposed is an important piece of the adaptation puzzle. I find that understanding is a dynamic skill, meaning that you cannot know and anticipate everything in advance of performance. However, if you understand some of what you will experience several weeks (at least two) in advance of the performance, you will be more able to act effectively when something new and unfamiliar comes your way in terms of a circumstance.

Internal Control

There is no surprise that control is also a pathway to effective adaptation. The operative word within the discussion is "effective". Sometimes athletes and their staff become bogged down in things they cannot control, and then try to control irrelevant factors, that should really have little influence on how the athlete performs. By focusing on irrelevant factors such as trying to intimidate an opponent when those sorts of things are just a waste of energy misdirects focus. Control is a relatively simple pathway to understand, though in understanding it, you need to also understand (1) that only some things can be controlled by you, (2) that others can be controlled by members of your working team, and (3) that only some factors are worthy of control, with others being irrelevant.

The first item worthy of control is you! There is lots of literature out there in sport psychology about aspects that fall within the discussion of self-control. People throw around terms like self-regulation, self-confidence, and self-determination when they begin to speak about matters of self-control. The bottom line is that without self-control, no other type of control that I will spell out directly beneath this paragraph, matters. Self-control is attempted through correct breathing techniques, because without adequate oxygen to your brain your thinking much like most other people's, will become muddled and misdirected. So, you can look to any mental training book and even some relaxation and guided meditation books to find strategies for effective breathing.

There are other strategies to use in the ring, but we will get to that topic later in the book when we speak about performance in the ring. Self-control also extends to strategies like progressive muscle relaxation, where a narrator (on a CD) guides you through a process of relaxation, starting often with your toes, and then progressing upward to your parts of your head and so, where you think. Progressive muscle relaxation (PMR) is to be used in the evening, the night before the fight, not to be mistaken with the night of the fight! The objective with PMR is to establish some relaxation before you go off to sleep. I have worked with several athletes who say they don't sleep well in the final night before the fight. If you struggle with sleep before a bout, PMR is a good starting place in terms of relaxation strategies.

Relaxation can also be achieved through visualization strategies. The strategy my athletes like most is called "the relaxation image". Each athlete has his / her own unique image that builds relaxation. For some, an image where you might be sitting on the beach is appealing, with toes in the sand, a warm sun, and a rolling ocean with a beautiful horizon. Others have chosen pictures where they were sitting on a dock in front of a fresh water lake, with loons calling, a sunset, and the sound of crickets. The neat thing about the relaxing image is that you already know what image will relax you. It could be a nature image, a crackling fire, or anything else that comes to your mind. Develop your relaxing image with as much detail as you can and choose an image based on an experience that relaxed you in the past.

Team Control

A great athlete is built and refined with the help of a great team. There was a time when I traveled with the Canadian Men's National Boxing Team. Without exception, when the team athletes were surrounded by a harmonious coaching and sport science staff they settled into their performances and delivered great results. It was not just about team harmony, though. The team staff covered all of the bases and attended to our athletes' needs so that they could focus exclusively on performance.

During the very same time, the national team that always outdid us was the Cuba National Team. Even from the outside, just watching those athletes and coaching staff prepare to do battle, it was evident that the athletes approached their international tournaments with a very simple approach. All that the athletes had to worry about were their performances. They trained in privacy, every athlete lined up for his massage at the right time before his warm-up, even their team clothing was intimidating. It seemed from the outside that their athletes led an even simpler and more focused life during tournaments than did our own. Knowing what I do now about how the Cuban Team was structured by their coaching staff, what I saw was the tip of a very sizable iceberg.

The athletes that our working team engage with know from the very beginning what role they need to lead and also when they need to step aside and let members of the working team cover off our respective tasks. Some athletes have a hard time letting go of the control, and we choose not to work with those sorts of athletes. Why? Because no athlete can control everything – not even the very best of athletes. The athletes who try to control everything burn out sooner or later. The important thing that every athlete needs to understand is that "no one makes it alone". Behind that statement, the people you surround yourself with have to know exactly what they are doing, and also how to coordinate their strengths with the strengths of the others in the working team. I recall working with one coach who was fantastic as a coach, but he could not coordinate his strengths with those of the people he surrounded himself with. With every athlete, and in no exception, his athletes eventually stumbled and fell. The athletes would relinquish the things that needed to be out of their control only to one person. The athlete and coach were performing at a very high level, and so, even the coach needed to assign things he was not well versed in to others in his team who could do the tasks even better than he could.

The bottom line is that you need to understand and believe that in order for you to be at your best, that some tasks should be managed by the people you surround yourself with. Next, you need to surround yourself with the right people, meaning people who have the skills to cover off the tasks that you should not be overseeing. Finally, when you let go of those items of control to those in your team, the right people have to take on the tasks, and the team members need to coordinate well in order to make certain that your needs are addressed by the team member best qualified to take on the task. For example, in our working team, it is my job as the sport psychology consultant and motivational coach to conduct a profile of our athlete's next opponent and bring that information back to the boxer. Though our head coach or our medical staff lead could likely do the job of profiling, I have the background in sport psychology research and so the most expertise in that area. Matters of nutrition go to the nutritionist, though with consultation from the medical staff lead person. Matters pertaining to tactics for the next fight are decided by the coaching staff, and not by sport science staff. If you look at great athletes with careers that have fallen apart, you will see promoters dabbling in coaching and corner discussions and sport agents serving as sport psychology consultants. Every person in the team has his role, and the rule of thumb is for the most qualified person in relation to the given task to do his job as a coordinated effort and as part of the larger team.

Now, you might be just starting to compete, and so your team might be comprised of a coach and maybe a few other members. The same rules apply regardless of the number of people involved in your team. Remember to let go of tasks that can be covered off better by someone else, make certain that the right person has taken on the task, and also ensure that your team works as a team!

On the other hand, you need to also pull your weight in the team. I have been witness to boxers who've assigned every single task to other people, including the packing of their own competition clothing before they leave to the competition venue. I recall too many cases both at the national team and professional levels when someone other than the athlete packed the athlete's bag. In fact, during the Super Six Tournament I watched one pre-bout episode where the boxer, a well respected and high quality boxer, left it to his team to bring his equipment to the venue. Next thing I witnessed was that the boxer arrived at the competition venue without his clothes. Most of the time, oversights are in relation to minute details such as a forgotten mouth guard or headgear. Some items need to be the responsibility of the boxer, and one of those responsibilities is packing your own clothing and making certain that it travels with you to the competition site. Another responsibility is that you are well rested before your bout. A third example is that you stay warm from the point you end your warm-up until the first bell. Those responsibilities are yours, and yours alone.

From what I know about aspects of personal and team control, when boxers and their team deviate outside of their respective roles and also choose to be sloppy and let important controllable things go, you – the boxer will eventually become over-loaded by stress. The result will be that you will not put forth a great performance, for the every reason that you were unable to adapt to the challenges in front of you.

Aspects Not Requiring Control

Directly above I have made a case for what things need to be controlled, and by whom. There are also athletes and coaching staff out there in the boxing world that lose their focus and as a result, start attending to unnecessary distractions, meaning things that are either irrelevant or uncontrollable. One prime example is that you cannot control how the opponent behaves before the fight. I have noticed with some of the opponents that my best athletes have fought have tried to pull my clients into a fight during the weigh-in or in the middle of a press conference. The two examples just provided are encountered only by high profile professional boxers. However, the general lesson of focusing on yourself and not your opponent is important. The best thing you can do is focus on yourself, and the worst thing you can do is place focus and energy outside of yourself.

I have also observed lots of cases where boxers have lost their focus just after the ring official made a bad or unfair call. A few days ago I watched a boxer on television whom I know quite well. The boxer was called for a low blow and the referee issued a warning. The call was questionable, and watching the fight proceed immediately after the call I was curious where the boxer's mind was – on the bout or on the recent – questionable call. About 15 seconds later, the opponent hit the boxer I knew with a very accurate temple shot. Next thing the boxer knew he was taking a knee and trying to clear his head. The remaining 40 seconds of the round was touch and go as the athlete tried to stay focused on the present – with questionable success. Happily, the athlete recovered in the rounds that followed and kept his world ranking.

The lesson you could draw from the story I just shared with you is that boxers, even some of the best known ones, sometimes lose their focus. When boxers lose their focus, it is not that the focus is lost. Rather, the focus is misdirected at the incorrect target – meaning outside of the immediate second and what needs to be executed right this split second! You need to focus on what you can control and accept what you and those around you cannot control. After all, to adapt and stay focused in the second, there are only a few things that really need your attention – the rest is irrelevant.

Self-enhancement

This past year, a documentary about Iron Mike Tyson was released. The documentary was beautifully written and pieced together so that you could get a real sense of what Iron Mike is about as a person and former boxer. Mike's meteoric rise to the top of the Heavyweight division was no surprise to anyone. When you watch footage of him on YouTube, especially the look on his face walking to the ring before the Trevor Berbick fight, or before the Michael Spinks fight, you see a boxer who is single-minded, focused and relentless. In both cases, neither opponent was able to make eye contact with Mike when they touched gloves just before the first bell. What followed, again, was of no surprise to those of us who've witnessed the footage of both fights. The outcome was very certainty from the first bell, forward to the very quick end result of knockouts.

To a certain point in his career, Tyson was extremely focused and well prepared. After a certain point however, he started taking short cuts. Less preparation was done in advance of fights, conditioning lacked, and as an end result unnecessary losses followed quickly. The thing about athlete adaptation is that athletes need to always engage in effortful preparation. Otherwise, even the most able of athletes, including Iron Mike, will eventually fall short in their efforts. Self-enhancement relates to the steps an athlete engages in to better himself. Those steps are explained through ongoing effort, directed in the right direction and from that effort, improved abilities.

I have worked on occasion with one athlete who became a world champion through careful management and extensive – grueling training. Though the athlete was not as sound as many world champions from boxing, he was aware of his limitations and so, made the very most of the skills and abilities he had. Sometimes good boxers become great boxers, just because they are effortful in their training, bout preparation, and bout execution. Often, the most talented of boxers are surpassed by more committed, better-managed opponents. In reality, ability in and of itself is necessary, but insufficient when it comes to a boxer's success. Ability without properly directed effort take an athlete only so far. For the rest of the journey, the athlete needs to work, and that work must be carefully thought out, and directed toward success.

There is also a time in every boxer's life when it is time to step down and make room for the next generation of boxers. Though some professional boxers try to fight father time, their abilities wane to the point that even with directed effort, they are only a shadow of their old selves. Without naming any names, there are a few such athletes found in professional boxing, today. Consequently, there are certain weaknesses that at a certain point, even the best of effort cannot overcome and offset. Effort and ability then, walk hand in hand. Without both pieces together, the athlete will never advance beyond a certain point, and so, he will not adapt well to the most challenging of circumstances, having left one of those pieces behind.

Trusting the Team

To this point in our discussion, all of the pieces that package into adaptation have mostly about you. Great performances result from great training contexts, working with coaches and support staff. No matter how good a working team is though, if they are not trusted, their roles are muted, meaning that their qualities are lost to distrust. I know of a great boxer who hopefully one day will be considered more than just an amazing prospect. The athlete has every resource at his fingertips, and yet he distrusts people – even the most trustworthy of people. I have observed the athlete from the outside, and on occasion tried to suggest things to him and his manager in terms of pulling together a comprehensive working team, with medical staff, sport science staff, and coaching staff. The athlete is reluctant of a comprehensive approach and from what I can tell, he trusts no one. Distrust can poison an athlete's mind and render him / her unprepared for important performances. As I have suggested, great athletes become great among great working teams. Granted not all people are trustworthy, but some are, and when you find them, integrate them as part of a coordinated effort.

As a boxer, I have suggested that there are times when you have to give up control to members of your working team. I would bet that for some athletes who have a challenge trusting others, it is very hard to give up control, even when it needs to be handed over to another person. The thing about trust, is that when you correctly trust people who can help you, you also free yourself to focus on the things you need to focus on, and nothing more.

The best performers have a simple approach to their performances. The way to a simple approach is to clean up all of clutter by letting go of control items you need to let go of. If you try to control everything, at a certain point you will become overwhelmed and your performance will suffer. So why trust? You need to trust others in order to really let go of unnecessary distractions and unnecessary tasks.

When my students and I have engaged in research with Olympic athletes and professional athletes, we found that the people who athletes tended to trust include the members of your working team, your teammates, your friends and your family. Now I must admit that not every one of those resources is always trustworthy, but some of them are. Family might help when you need to discuss a personal matter or seek help with another family member, such as a child. Family can lighten the load by covering for you as you ramp up for an important performance. Friends outside of boxing can serve as an outlet when you take some hours away from boxing related tasks. One of my boxers has close friends he grew up with. A few of those friends have helped him with business decisions, as a sounding board away from the boxing context. It seems in his case that his friends do the trick and that they are extremely loyal and caring. There are other boxers I have witnessed who at a certain point are surrounded by so many friends that it is hard to determine which one are real friends versus hangers on. Good friends always will guide you toward peaceful decisions, improved relations with the people you work, and so, better performance. Teammates and sparring partners should also have your best interest at heart. I know of one boxer who went off to a training camp to assist a well-known boxer in his pre-bout preparation for a world title. The sparring partner went into the sparring (on salary by the elite boxer) and proceeded to knock him down, intentionally. Teammates are a very important piece to the adaptation puzzle, but they have to be trusted members of the team, first and foremost. If they are trusted, they will help you prepare for the upcoming performance and work with you in your best interest.

As you can see there are lots of resources for you to choose from. Now even if those resources have your best interest in mind, they must also be trustworthy, or in this case creditable. I have observed many an athlete guided by well-intentioned friends who knew nothing about boxing. Even though the friends were trustworthy in terms of their intentions, they were also untrustworthy in terms of their level of knowledge to address the topic of discussion pursued by the athlete. It is one thing to be loyal and another to be knowledgeable. The trustworthy resources you need to seek out must meet both characteristics.

Belonging in the Group

The final piece of the puzzle is belonging – meaning how you fit within your working team. When you work with coaches and sport science staff for example, they must mesh with you, but you also must mesh with them. There are athletes out there in the world today, pursuing excellence at a very high level. Some of those athletes see the people who are helping them as part of their team, while also seeing themselves as the center of that team. There are also other athletes who isolate themselves from their working team, perhaps due to a lack of trust. The athletes seem to stand alone, and only come together with their working group for training. The best of teams have a bi-directional sense of belonging with the athletes and their support staff belonging to each other. In those working conditions, great performances most often result – especially over the long-term. My favorite athletes are the ones who run with their working team, are able to hang out and watch movies, and really contribute to that sense of shared purpose. The athletes I really do not enjoy working with create environments where there is an "us" and "them" environment between the athlete and their support staff.

The athletes who separate themselves don't last as long as they should in the sport, primarily because they way they go about their business takes the fun right out of the sport. The working staff tends to dislike working with those sorts of athletes because the athletes deplete energy that should be devoted to bettering the athlete and preparing him/her for the challenges that lay ahead. Each of us only has so much energy to expend each day and that energy must be harnessed and directed in the right direction. When the working team is compelled to constantly re-direct the athlete toward a more positive attitude and the topic is re-visited time and again, it becomes hard for the working team to feel invested in the athlete's development.

So what to do? The athletes my working team and I commit to are few and far between. Those athletes are fun to work with, committed toward excellence, and they also bring positive energy to the team. They carry their weight in enthusiasm and conviction and I find that what the athlete puts out, he gets back in spades. If you are not really investing effort and enthusiasm in your working team, you are misdirected your energy and also, losing time. There is no time to waste – you need to bring vigor and kindness into your team, because much of what your working team brings to the table is selfless. The team you have surrounded yourself with are there for you! You need to remember who you are and also make space in your team for those investing in you to enjoy themselves. I know that as an athlete you are the center of the discussion, and so you should be! However, with no team, there is no athlete. You need take the time and tune in to what your team is doing for you and see if you can come up with ways to add energy and momentum into your working group. In doing so, you are investing in your team unselfishly. In response though, you will be invested in your own training and performance environment. When you need those members most, there will be lots of credit to cash in on.

SO WHAT'S NEXT?

I will bet that you are probably thinking: "wow, there is lots of information to make sense of if I want to learn adaptation skills". Adaptation is actually a comprehensive approach to training and competition. Chances are you are already doing a fair amount of the five pathways spelled out to you in this chapter. From our discussion though, you need to make sure to cover all of the basis so that you can perform correctly in the face of stressors like a heavy training load, a challenging tournament or opponent, or the progression to a higher level of competition.

People who adapt well are not necessarily the better athletes among us, though being talented is always helpful. However, as I have suggested, talent without correctly directed effort is relatively useless at a certain point in an athlete's development. Sooner or later athletes do need to learn how to manage stressors through their own strategies and also with the support staff who help out with training and development, such as coaching staff. When stressors are managed effectively, you will find that you can respond to tough challenges by increasing your effort, where others who you encounter might become overwhelmed.

Keep at your adaptation pathways and work on each one when you feel it is lacking a little. At times you might need to work on your relationships with those there to help you through the pathways of trusting and belonging. Other times you might need to work on your understanding, both of yourself and the challenges that you are about to face. Through understanding, you can develop good control and self-enhancement strategies to act upon your challenges in an ideal way.

The thing about adaptation is that you will never really master it across challenges. You will learn the skills and use those skills correctly in the moment. However, you need to keep adapting, and always remember that each challenge is dynamic and it could change on a moment's notice. Also, challenges might vary from one event to the next. Stay sharp, continue to work on your adaptation skills, and I promise you a level of success beyond that of most, if not all of your opponents.

FINAL REFLECTIONS

Adaptation is comprised of five pathways, understanding, control, self-enhancement, trusting, and belonging. Each of these five pathways will take you much closer to an effective adaptation strategy, when you need it in relation to a sport challenge, such as a tough tournament. When you anticipate a stressful situation, start your adaptation process with the pathway that you need most right now. The starting point that takes you toward effective adaptation can be any one of the pathways – assuming that you use it with care and detail. Once you have started on the path to adaptation, tie in additional pathways, as you need them. Remember that personal or interpersonal pathways are great in and of themselves. However, you need personal resources and also support from those around you to really adapt to a stressor. Do not take on any stressor on your own!

If you look at some of the better boxers in the amateur and professional ranks, and consider them in relation to the adaptation process we have just discussed, you will be better able to explain their rise to the top and for some, also their decline. Great athletes have great talent, but they also require a correct focus and good decisions along the way. If you understand, control, and self-enhance in relation to stressors that you need to tackle head on, and you respond with a logical plan, you will surpass your challenges and leave them in the dust.

On the other hand, if you are one of the many who focuses on far too many things, some of which you cannot control, you will overload yourself with stress. The result will be that your performance will suffer and so too, will your confidence. There is no time like the present to really think about what your next big challenge is, how you would like to adapt, and then, where to begin.

Chapter 9

PRE-BOUT CONFIDENCE

Some years ago I worked with a very talented professional athlete who was on the brink of greatness. The athlete had a tremendous amateur pedigree, meaning that his record at high-level amateur boxing tournaments included many medals. Eventually, the boxer decided to turn professional, and for a while he moved up the ranks to the point where was ranked among all of the associations, including the WBC, IBF, WBA, and WBO. On paper many anticipated that the boxer was on his way to a great and lucrative professional boxing career. Sadly, the athlete never did become a world champion, though he did come very close a few times, often against lesser opponents.

The story that I have just shared with you, though one I observed and know about, is not uncommon among many prospects found in professional boxing, past and present. Just because an athlete is promising does not necessarily mean that he or she will make it to the very top of the game. There are several aspects that need to also be in place such as good management and timing. In addition to the logistics required, boxers must also have that intangible characteristic that we like to regard as "confidence".

Coaches often think that athletes either have the "X Factor" of confidence, or they don't. I guess to some degree that belief is correct. Some athletes, either by chance or by some form of structure, build their confidence to that point where they can overcome odds and surpass better opponents. Recently, I was part of a working team where a boxer overcame the odds and beat a Ring Magazine Pound for Pound boxer, when the odds were more than 4-1 against our client. Those who bet for the favorite underestimated the importance of confidence in relation to significant bouts such as world-title bouts.

You will have your own tests along the way as you develop into a better, or perhaps a great boxer. If you want to move upwards in performance each time you are tested by a challenge, you will need a good dose of confidence, each time that stands up to the challenge in front of you. Confidence is not one of those things that either athletes have, or don't have. Instead, it is a skill that you need to develop through personal strategies and also through an extremely supportive, though challenging training and competition environment.

So, let's return to the belief of some people that confidence is something that athletes either have, or don't have. I am happy to say that based on sound evidence from within sport and also from general psychology, that confidence is a framework, and therefore a skill set that needs to be built into your development. Confidence is created through carefully designed training, correctly chosen competition, and obviously, also the highly important debriefing strategies that we will discuss toward the end of this book in Chapter 14. For now, let's turn our attention to what confidence is and generally, how it works.

CONFIDENCE AS A FRAMEWORK

Confidence relates to your belief, both in yourself and in those found in your environment. Self-confidence related to your belief in self is termed self-confidence. More general confidence extends beyond your belief in self, also to those positioned to support you in your boxing efforts, such as your coaches, sport psychologist, nutritionist, strength and conditioning coach, etc. Both types of (self and general) confidence are extremely important, and you need each in order to really succeed and bet at your best.

The interesting thing about confidence is that it is not one of those things that you either have, or don't have. I have heard many a coach or athlete believe that some athletes are born with confidence and others just aren't. The reality is that you might have confidence in one circumstance, and not have it when needed in another. You might also have confidence in relation to one opponent, but that confidence might dissolve when you face a second opponent. Below, I will walk you through how to create your confidence systematically, based upon a sound body of literature first created by a social psychologist from Stanford University, Albert Bandura. What follows is the general framework, taken from the abstract to the boxing environment.

Confidence operates in three related ways that each help explain the larger picture why you might or might not have large amounts of confidence in a given circumstance, such as an important bout or tough sparring. Those aspects are termed "strength of confidence", "level of confidence", and the "generality of confidence."

Strength of Confidence

In a given moment we have a specific amount of confidence. The amount of confidence in that given moment refers to how strong our confidence is right then. I have watched many a boxer on his/her walk to the ring and looked at the facial expressions during those dramatic moments. If you carefully observe a fighter's facial expressions as he/she is walking to the ring, you will learn a lot about how confident they are right then. Some have a hard focus much like Mike Tyson did when he walked to the ring, when he was at his best. In the moments before he first claimed a world title against Trevor Berbick, it was abundantly clear to the commentators and to the audience just how confident Mike was in those immediate pre-bout moments. Not long after, Tyson unified the titles, fighting against Michael Spinks. Again, Tyson was extremely focused and to the outside observer, he was very confident and ready for the task.

Now, compare Tyson's facial expression before each of the aforementioned bouts with his opponents. Trevor Berbick and Michael Spinks both held an amateur pedigree as Olympians, and both were at that juncture in their professional careers, world champions. And yet, neither athlete looked confident in those final pre-bout moments. Neither boxer held Tyson's eye contact and what followed next was that both opponents were cautious in the opening second of Round One. If you look back to the bouts of both vanquished athletes in the bouts before they lost to Tyson, both were extremely different people, in terms of their confidence.

The amount of confidence you have in those critical moments is extremely important if you want to be a performer and bring out the very best in yourself. For you personally, that amount of confidence you hold will determine whether you are active or passive in your battle plan. If you let things happen, things can slip away from you in a hurry. Your plan can dissolve into nothing but thin air and slowly, you will be pulled into the plan of your opponent. Strength in confidence determines your commitment to your plan, just as you are executing it.

Your opponent will notice how much confidence you have in those crucial moments and seconds of a fight. It will be as visible to him/her as it is to most any other observer. However, for your opponent, those early emotional signs that you will be on or off of your game will influence his amount of confidence, either confirming it, or testing it. So, the amount of confidence you have plays as a double-edged sword. It can enhance your performance and take away from the present amount of your opponent's confidence, assuming you have lots of confidence at the right moment and second! The second side of the sword is that if you have only a small – fragile amount of confidence when you need that confidence most, not only will you feel that something is missing, your opponent will feed off of your self-doubt.

As you might have guessed, confidence is a valuable commodity to you, the boxer. There is no such thing as a permanently confident boxer, even if you are Mike Tyson, Miguel Cotto, Juan Manuel Marquez, or one of the Klitchko brothers. It is easy enough to be confident eight weeks away from an important fight. Eight weeks from the critical fight you might be perfectly confident and in that moment, your confidence would clearly be "strong". However, moments, hours, and days can change your confidence, either for worse or better.

Some athletes and coaches live on cruise control and then find themselves in the fight of their lives against a relentless opponent. Not long ago, an unnamed world champion was fighting a very tough – persistent opponent. For the first six or so rounds, the champion moved about the ring with wonderful footwork and lateral movement. All the while, the champion taunted the opponent and made him miss. The champion's confidence in the early rounds during the bout was extremely strong. Slowly but surely though, the opponent closed the physical distance and by the tenth round people were on the edge of their seats. The champion seemed to deflate and near the very end of the fight, the champion was knocked to the canvass. Tough opponents tend to wear down even the best of champions and they do so systematically, second by second, moment by moment. Such athletes know that confidence can waiver from one second to the next if the boxer is not focused and so intelligent boxers persist in their focus and at the same time break the spirit – momentary confidence of their opponent.

Level of Confidence

Confidence is not one of the things that you necessarily can expect regardless of the opponent - test in front of you. Even a world champion can be confident against one opponent or in one arena only to find that confidence tested and even reduced when circumstances and opponents change. Arthur Abraham, also known as King Arthur is a fantastic defensive fighter. For several years, opponents would travel from most everywhere to Germany in order to challenge Abraham. People believed that Abraham had an abundance of confidence, so much so that he would be able to challenge any boxer in his weight division, anywhere! The first fight in the ShowTime Super Six Tournament featured a highly confident Abraham against Jermain Taylor. Abraham prepared for the fight, clearly against an athlete on the decline. In the latter rounds of the fight, Abraham opened up his offense and knocked out Taylor in one of the most dramatic KOs of 2009.

Soon after, Taylor moved onward to his second fight against Andre Dirrell, a young and talented boxer in his own right. Watching the documentaries leading up to the bout, Abraham was less focused. He visited the arena where the bout would take place and commented on how small it was. As the bout drew closer, suffered a delay, and was then re-scheduled, we saw an entirely different athlete in Abraham. By the time fight night arrived he was less confident. From the outside, I am not certain whether Dirrell troubled Abraham, but it was clear that fighting away from home was quite an adjustment.

It is one thing to fight in a simple familiar performance setting, such as in one's hometown. It is a far different task to exceed expectations on the road, when the venue is unfamiliar and the logistics surrounding the fight or tournament are very much out of the athlete and coach's control. So, fighting at home requires one level of confidence for the opponent who is comfortable in his own arena. Fighting away from home for the very same athlete becomes an entirely different level of challenge.

Opponents can also test one's confidence. I have witnessed many a world-class athlete look perfectly confident against a journeyman only to look unrecognizably smaller and less confident against a real opponent. There are such things as paper champions and lineal – real champions. People like Max Kellerman from HBO speak about real champions as those who seek out the most challenging tests and then bring their "A Game" to every test and every opponent. It is easy to look like a champion and flaunt your confidence when the opponent is weaker than you are. It is another thing to push out a great performance against the best of opponents as Jean Pascal did recently against Chad Dawson as the two young lions fought for the Ring Magazine Light Heavyweight Belt.

In amateur and professional boxers, some coaches and athletes are under the mistaken belief that protecting an athlete and retaining one's title is the most important thing. There are world champions from the past, though also among the alphabet world champions of today (the people who hold titles in one of the world boxing councils, associations, or organizations) who focus on cherry picking their opponents. In the short-term the athletes who benefit from such strategies retain their stature, but even they eventually realize that their stature is over-inflated. Champions are exposed all of the time, and the reason for many of the "exposures" results from over-protection. Boxers must be developed and tested at each level, right up to the highest level. Even at the highest level, boxers need to be carefully prepared and then tested to really know that they are on their game. "Stepping up" in class of opponent if correctly planned for will produce the most resilient of boxers – meaning those that have an illustrious career.

Generality of Confidence

Your confidence can also be built or reduced as a result of your experiences not only in sport, but also in life. When a boxer steps up to a new level of opponent or tournament, she/he likely feels a little stressed. The reason for that stress is a degree of unfamiliarity, meaning concern over the unknown. I have traveled many times with one national amateur boxing team to important world tournaments. When boxers travel to their first Pan-American of Olympic Games, many often report feeling overwhelmed. How possibly could qualifying competitions ever prepare the boxer for the high profile and complex sport environment of a profound tournament experience? Similarly, when I have worked with boxers in their first world title fight, as the fight draws closer I find that often, the athletes become a little panicked over what is at stake.

You would be somewhat correct if you were to think that nothing prepares a boxer for big steps upward in challenge. Clearly, the boxer who is performing for the first time at an Olympics has no Olympic experience to draw on. Similarly, the boxer fighting for the first time in a career also has no real – tangible boxing performances to draw on other than sparring. In such cases, coaches and athletes often take a leap of faith and just do their best. People have to start somewhere, and so there is always a beginning.

When we see a new experience as unique and so far different from any experience that came before it, there is a clear disconnect, meaning a million miles from what was experienced before this new challenge and the present test. If you view new experiences as entirely disconnected from previous experiences you are actually doing yourself a disservice. Experiences in life always connect to other experiences that came before them – you just need to look for what connections exist. For example, a boxer on the brink of a world title bout might not have fought for a world title, but he/she did have experiences that were monumental in life before the present bout. How were these sport and life challenges handled, especially those that were handled with great success?

Believe it or not there are connections and consistencies in the way people handle pressure effectively in and outside of the ring. Questions of self-doubt don't just happen for the first time in relation to the bout in front of you. You have also experienced self-questioning at times in your past and managed to fight back and overcome your fears and concerns. The challenges you overcame in monumental moments can be found in your personal life, in your life as a student, and in your life as an employee. How you effectively overcame challenges and stressors in the past is exactly what you need to press into action in the present.

Instead of minimizing the amazing life experience you have gained over the years by saying that this situation is "different" from anything you experienced so far, realize that there are many life experiences that were at once different until they became familiar. Yes, you have to start somewhere in each aspect of your life, but how you need to effectively approach the challenging and unfamiliar experiences in front of you ought to be influenced by how you have managed tough tests in the past. Stay true to who you are, what has worked for you in the past, and you will find that your confidence will stand up to the test of time in and outside of the ring.

STRATEGIES THAT BUILD CONFIDENCE

There are some general strategies that you can use to further develop your confidence. Confidence is one of those things that can always be added to and as you now know, it needs to be built in relation to each challenge.

Useful Personal Experiences

I am often amazed when high performance boxers step up in opposition or tournament level. Few are the athletes who right away, take their skills with them onward to that next level. More often than not, the boxers lower their performance level and see to shrink at least a little when in the face of adversity. Recently, I traveled with a professional boxer who fought for a world title in another country. The boxer was undefeated to that point and the opponent in front of him was definitely beatable. I knew the client for more than a decade and so I was aware of how he looked before and during his professional bouts.

As the week before the fight moved forward, meaning fight night was drawing closer, the client seemed to lose his timing a little. To my eye there were certain indications that he was not fully comfortable with the strategy. This minor shift of second guessing his strategy was something new to the athlete. Typically he was very confident and he was able to fully integrate the suggestions if his head coach. So what was the difference before this fight in particular? The boxer was not really stepping up in opponent, but he was stepping up in terms of the stature of the fight, while also traveling to a foreign country to fight for the title. There were lots of unknowns before the fight and brought together, those unknowns reduced a great athlete to the level of a very good athlete, meaning a step downward in quality.

The end outcome was predictable, though better than it is for most other athletes experiencing the similar challenges of stepping up while traveling. He lost the bout 115-113 by two of the three judges, meaning he lots the bout by one round to a more experienced boxer, who happened to be boxing in his own home town. Though a loss for some people is nothing but a loss, the boxer came out of the fight with some very good insights and he is now taking his recent experience and his knowledge from the bout as he rebuilds for what will likely be a world title success this coming year.

There is no denying that personal experiences are the most important source of information to draw from when you are looking for a confidence boost. Regardless of what level you are, there are lessons you could take from the previous level, and carry forward to your new level of performance. If you are a methodical and disciplined athlete, and you have been that sort of athlete from several years now, keep those skills and they will be a strong foundation as you step up in class. Things that sharpen you are one level, will also sharpen you at the next level. Remember, you are a boutique operation and what works for you needs to be built upon and not abandoned.

On the other hand, there are also past experiences that might have worked in the past, that need to be improved upon at your new level of performance. Bad habits can only take you so far as an athlete. For example, eating the incorrect foods and then dropping weight radically in the final few days before you box can weaken you. Against low quality opposition there really little consequence to some bad habits, but eventually bad decisions cost you. The reality is that you need to learn before it is too late what habits are good habits versus bad habits, and then look to maintain the good habits and replace the bad ones with better decisions. To be a great boxer, you need to become self-aware, meaning supportive of yourself when you have earned that right and also critical when you are straying from decisions that could help you move forward as an athlete.

My suggestion is that you maintain tapes of yourself where you boxed well and watch what you did, not only during the bout, but also in your walk to the ring, the minute in between rounds, etc. Remind yourself that you have lots of great experiences banked, and use only your better performances as examples of "what to do". There are also lessons that can be gained from mistakes, but we will get to that point later in the book when we consider post-performance evaluations in Chapter Fourteen.

Observations Teammates and Opponents of Like Mind and Ability

Just as you could learn lots by referring back to your own great performances, you could also look to the performances of other boxers when seeking to build your confidence. Recently, I worked with an extremely tall heavyweight boxer. The boxer is an intellectual, his style is very traditional European, as he fights off of his back heal and likes to jab from a distance. You would recognize this type of athlete – he is extremely upright, has good stiff jab, and a lean body. When you think of great boxers who are similar and in the same weight division who comes to mind? For me, the Klitchko brothers exemplify intelligent boxing from the outside and the correct use of the jab, by tall, lean boxers of European style. So, I suggested to the athlete that he watch footage of the two brothers from their previous amateur and professional bouts.

If you visit YouTube, you will find lots of useful footage that you can draw on. Simply type in the name of a boxer of similar style to you, but one that really captures the type of skills you would like to press into action. Watch the athlete and really dissect / break down what he/she is doing and then experiment with the techniques with your coach. Experimentation should obviously start with shadow boxing and transition upward in difficulty to sparring and then into progressively challenging fights.

Observations build confidence in another way, also. Several years ago I traveled with a national boxing team to an important high profile tournament. I was told repeatedly before the tournament not to expect too much from our athletes as the national team record for that particular tournament was three medals and five wins by a team of twelve boxers. In advance of the tournament we developed a team cheer that all of the athletes came together for before each boxer's performance. The cheer was a sort of send off for the boxer before he performed.

When the first few athletes won their fights in the first days of the two-week tournament, the other athletes supported and also watched the successes of their friends. With the first few wins, the team caught fire and our boxers started to believe that they could also win a fight. After each day's performances, we had a team meeting and we debriefed the day's events. All of the discussions were built around topics of focusing and re-focusing as the athletes moved deeper into the tournament. Before long, eight athletes won their bouts, then we were up to ten and then twelve wins. Even the coaches and long-established team manager began to believe in the possibility of winning. As the team members watched each other win, team members seemed to leap frog from win to win, and day-to-day, until at the very end of the tournament, seventeen wins and seven medals resulted. In short, the increase in wins and medals was more than a two hundred percent increase in performance from the team's previous best ever performance.

Why do you think that memorable experience happened? Was it simply a lucky tournament and a matter of being in the right place at the right time, or was there more to those wins than coincidence? When we see people who are our friends and teammates moving beyond what we initially believed as possible, we tend to follow them into the great unknown and dare to extend our expectations to a higher standard of performance. As people of similar abilities and background move forward to the next level, we start to wonder whether we, also, can move to that level and be more than we initially anticipated.

If you do not have the opportunity that the national team members above have of being in that magical team environment, you can still use your observational skills to build your confidence. What separates an A+ student from a B student is not always a matter of ability. Similarly, what separates a great boxer from a good boxer is not just a matter of schooling or talent. Observations of others, providing they are of similar skills, body type and level, can provide you with some hope that if they can achieve, so can you.

Supportive Words and Actions From Others

I have listened to coaches work corners in between rounds. On far too many occasions I have heard comments like "come on, be yourself", "work harder", "stop being sloppy", and other general comments that are all met by a confused boxer. People often think they are being supportive of another's performance, but only in some cases are they really effective in what they do. Think for a second about the sorts of things that help you with performance. What should feedback sound like? Who should be delivering the feedback? How should it be delivered? These are only a few of the examples that build into the importance of supportive words and actions from others.

I recall two very talented amateur boxers changing coaches because the coach they were initially working with could not provide effective feedback in the corner in between rounds during international tournaments. The kinds of feedback that boxers need collapse into two categories: very specific - tightly worded suggestions about how to do a certain skill, or praise. Tightly worded directives need to happen during sparring and in between rounds of a fight. Boxers only have so much time to absorb feedback, often times in a minute when they are likely a little winded and so, in the process of recovering before the next round. In some cases the feedback confirms what you are already doing, in other instances there are also suggestions of what to modify. When coaches provide more than ten words of explanation, you likely aren't able to absorb all of the details, and so the words are lost on you. Then you step back into the ring all the while struggling to remember the precise details your coach has suggested to you.

Have you ever tried to cram just before an exam or an important interview of some sort? How much detail do you remember as you cram information during the final minute before the important performance ahead? I would bet you could remember a handful of words and nothing more! A perfect example of carefully chosen words by a head coach is exemplified by watching Freddie Roach, who works with Manny Pacquiao and Amir Khan. Though I have never met Freddie Roach, I marvel at his ability to provide succinct feedback that his athletes seem to understand and then effectively press into action in their next round. So, feedback in the corner from your coach needs to be very clear and tightly worded into only a few words.

Next, the delivery of those words needs to be provided slowly, clearly, and only when you are ready to take them in. Some boxers like to take a few deep breaths and then have a drink before they receive their feedback. Others like to catch their breath, receive the feedback and then have their drink of water. Only you know what sequence works best for you. You also know how much information you can absorb and how it should be delivered. If you have yet to think about what sort of communication approach works best for you, give it some thought and work on capturing the perfect approach. Experiment with your boxer-coach communication in sparring and see how much information you are retaining. If the answer is that you have perfect retention, meaning that you could remember everything, then the approach you have works for you. If on the other hand, the approach you are presently using is less than perfect, work with your coach and refine it!

Finally, feedback and motivation doesn't just happen in the corner or only by a coach. Support can be provided by a teammate, another coaching staff member, a sport psychology consultant or someone else in your team. You will find that there is no end of people willing to provide you with feedback, especially as you develop into an elite boxer. You need to consider very carefully whom you should listen to and what people should not be given much attention. I have noticed with some high profile boxers that as they progress in their careers, people surface out of the woodwork and try to attach themselves. At the end of the day, only the influence of certain support staff will help you with your skills and also with your confidence. Those athletes who find themselves surrounded by large entourages of groupies often eventually suffer the consequences of following the wrong advice. Only knowledgeable – creditable people can effectively support you. When your decisions are built from good decisions built upon good guidance, the result will be a solid level of confidence, built upon substance.

Self-control Strategies

The final piece to the puzzle is that you can also build confidence by taking control of yourself. You would be surprised how important self-control is to your self-confidence. Take for example the boxer who is walking to the ring for an important point, all the while chest breathing on that walk. By the time the athlete arrives at the ring he will likely feel out of breath, weak, and so, concerned that he won't be able to perform as well as he can. Chest breathing is a very common habit (notice I didn't call chest breathing a problem) just before performance for athletes who are overwhelmed. Consider this: how possibly can an athlete feel confident and energized if he/she cannot control the most basic of skills – breathing?

The reality is that there are things you can control, things that others can control, and things that are just uncontrollable. The things that you can control include your breathing, your wellbeing, your attitude, self-discipline, focusing, and re-focusing. The most basic piece of those just provided is breathing. Correct, deep breathing requires you to breath in through your nose (if possible) and breath out through your mouth. When you look to take a deep breath, consider the sort of breathing you do when you are most relaxed. In those moments, you will find that your stomach rises and falls to a rhythm. In a sense, you are actually taking in so much oxygen that your stomach rises to make space for a lung, filled to its capacity with air. With the large amount of air taken in to your lungs, you are able to think your way through most any problem, look at the possible solutions, and select the most effective one.

When boxers return to the corner after a tough round of sparring or enter the ring, in either case taking shallow breaths, what happens is that they rob themselves of the air needed to think clearly. If you the problem of limited air supply is something you are familiar with, you might not be depleting yourself intentionally, but you are depleting yourself of air just the same! Start taking control of yourself by first and foremost controlling your breathing. Everything starts with a deep breath and proceeds from that point, forward.

From breathing you will then be able to make sense of the challenges that are in front of you. Remember that people who panic first stop breathing. If only they chose to take a deep breath. Be different, take a deep breath and then see how a challenge that was first confusing becomes much clearer. Control always begins with breathing and from that point you can go forward and work on other self-control strategies that match with the circumstances you are presently in.

If you are trying to focus before an important day of training, take a few deep breaths as you are walking into the ring and then re-visit the goals you set for that day's training, as discussed in Chapter Four. If you are a little flat or overly relaxed before a day's training, take a few deep breaths and then as you begin your warm-up work on elevating your heart rate. Combining focus on your goals with an elevated heart rate will bring you into the present and help you become fully engaged in this moment's training.

If you are working on a warm-up for a very important bout and you find that you are feeling a little overwhelmed, begin with the breathing described above and always take in 4-5 deep breaths before making any snap decision about how you feel. In this case, first breathe, and then make your good decisions. Next, continue to breath as you inch closer to the final minutes just before the fight. As you enter the ring, take a few deep breaths, each time moving your hands toward the floor and then take that deep breath as you slowly raise your hands toward the arena's ceiling. Only after you have taken a few deep breaths should you look to the crowd, acknowledge the judges, and then lock eyes with your opponent. Again, control comes from clarity of thinking, and clarity of thinking comes from good breathing decisions.

TAKING YOUR CONFIDENCE TO THE RING

When you step into the ring to perform, you do so based on your preparation. Some of that preparation is built from realizing that you have methods that have worked for you in the past in challenging situations. You know what you must do and the critical thing is for you to do what works best for you. To make good decisions you need to first acknowledge that you have made good decisions in the past, and then understand how to repeat those decisions and apply them to your immediate challenge. Far too often people abandon what works best for them by looking at their immediate challenge as something that is unique and completely different from anything they have experienced to this point. Though challenges might be different, the one common factor in the situation is you and as a boutique operation, you have specific things that work best for you – press them into action.

As you are challenged by a task that is out of the ordinary, you might see yourself as alone in the challenge. Many high quality professional boxers eventually fight for an important title, especially if they are well managed. When many of my clients fought for world titles for the first time, they found that nothing fully prepared them for the possibility of becoming a world champion. The task of having to fight for that monumental world title held lots of pressure beyond just over-coming an opponent. At the end of the bout in front of them would possibly be a profound title, a change in financial status, and really, a significant potential change to their life. In those months of training leading up to the monumental event, one of the things that those athletes sometimes considered is that there were other boxers who became world champions before them. The reality is that the experience you are now facing has likely been experienced by someone else with an equivalent story and series of experiences to your own. I have suggested visiting YouTube and learning from how others have overcome similar life challenges. Who knows, you might learn something while also finding useful strategies. Instead of re-investing the wheel, look to the positive similar experiences of other boxers and then tweak them with your coach to match with who you are.

The environment you choose to surround yourself with also has a profound influence on your potential to succeed. I have been witness to many talented boxers; only some who chose to surround themselves with a good working team, meaning good advisors. It is not enough to have fantastic talent. Talent will overcome many opponents and likely take you to a certain point in a boxing career – just not the full distance to a long-term success story. A fantastic working team can help you make good decisions about what fights to take and they can also help you right through the bout with good useful advice when you need it most. If you surround yourself with great people, you must also then take the next step and listen carefully to what they say. You also have a say in the decisions that are being made, but as the challenge draws nearer you need to stick with your team, and work with them toward the same objectives: winning, while at the same time also progressing.

Finally, all the work in preparation for the fight by yourself and your working team needs to be solidified by good self-control strategies on your part. All the schooling and preparation in advance of the fight can be taken away by something so simple as ineffective – incorrect breathing habits. You need to take control of the challenge in front of you by first taking control of yourself at the most basic level: breathing. Breathe and then think clearly. Make the right decisions, and know that from good breathing, better decisions will become likely.

FINAL REFLECTIONS

Confidence is one of the most fundamental skills that any boxer needs, daily. The interesting thing about confidence is that it is one of those dynamic skills that can come and go, depending on your preparation, focus, and self-discipline. Three months in advance of an important bout, any boxer can look confident. In the final minutes leading up to a fight is a different story, with only the most resilient and deeply confident of athletes standing up to the acid test of performance. Mike Tyson correctly stated that every boxer has a plan until they get hit. He is correct, and to his statement I would add that the most well-prepared and resilient athletes have plans for when they get hit, also.

Moving forward, you need to work on your confidence each day. Confidence is not one of those taken for granted things that you can just assume will surface when you need it. As you have seen in this chapter, the skill of confidence needs to be systematically developed and pressed into action. More times than not, your opponents will not have a systematic approach to help build their confidence. What I am proposing here is that you can! Take the time each day to cover off at least two of the four confidence strategies and chip away at these strategies. Knowing that you have taken good steps forward each day, when you finally do step into the ring against a tough opponent, you will find yourself standing on a very solid foundation.

The opposite though, also holds true. There are very promising professional athletes who've been featured in high profile boxing magazines such as The Ring – my favorite. Some of these athletes are protected to their own demise and are far too slow in stepping up to the next level of opponent. The reason why such athletes are held back, either due to personal reasons or the intuition of their working teams, is because something seems to be missing. What sort of something do you think is missing from those athletes, who in this book will remain nameless? That something, of X Factor at the end of the day is confidence.

Chapter 10

STUDYING YOUR OPPONENT IN ADVANCE

Up to this point in the book, lots of energy and emphasis has been placed on preparing you for a high standard of boxing performance. There is no denying that much of that preparation is about you, how you train, who you surround yourself with, and what you do leading up and then in performance. Boxing is one of those sports where you perform in relation to an opponent. This chapter is devoted to a topic often times left untouched by sport authors. We are going to talk about how to study your opponent and then, how to use what you know.

No one is a better example of how to get into the mind of the opponent than Muhammad Ali in the 1970s and 1980s and also, Bernard Hopkins, especially from 2001 onward through 2010. Both of these boxers were fantastic students of boxing. They are prime examples of great fighters, and some of their instincts took them into parts of the sport that extended well beyond the studying of opponent footage. Both of these athletes were able to understand their opponents and then break those opponents down, or soften the opponents up. Bottom line: Ali and Hopkins were able to gain the upper hand through intelligent profiling of their opponents.

Today, we are on the very cusp of a more scientific approach to boxing. Old school ways bring a lot in terms of boxer self-discipline. However, some things have changed and you will see more of the better boxers starting to profile their opponents. Doing so doesn't just happen by chance. Rather, profiling of the opponent requires a systematic approach that you need to do with the help of a strong working team that includes you, and you're your managers, coaches and a sport psychology consultant.

Together, you and your team can learn what to expect from your opponent with ample time to develop proactive and reactive strategies to counter and reduce his/her strengths. People live and perform with their habits, through a solid education of your opponent, you can develop refined skills for your next fight, built from evidence instead of guess work and a general preparation. Confidence and know how are built from fact and some of those facts comes from what can be learned about your opponent.

What follows is some of my approach to studying your opponent. I will share with you some starting points that will really get you thinking about the power of understanding your opponent. Remember that these skills should not be the entire focus of your pre-bout preparation. However, you are preparing in relation to the opponent. And so, let's prepare in part based on who will be in front of you – the opponent.

FIGHT RECORD

There is much that you could learn from your opponent's fight record. Though numbers sometimes do lie and mislead in boxing, records are a very good starting point. Start with the sheer number of bouts the opponent has performed in. If the number is high, then obviously the athlete has some experience behind him/her. Look beyond the numbers to wins and losses and you start getting a sense of what sorts of experiences serve as the foundation in terms of what the opponent will bring to the ring. There are very talented athletes in training who simply never learn how to rise to the challenge of performance. On the other hand, if the opponent has a relatively small number of bouts under his belt to this point, that too is worth knowing. Opponents with less experience can become unhinged because they might not have encountered your style, strategy, and tactics.

Look further into the opponent's record and part of what you will find includes KO percentages, meaning how often the athlete has stopped his/her opponents. There are some well-known athletes with high KO percentages with a certain pattern in terms of when they score their KOs. Some with relatively high percentages achieve their KOs in the latter part of rounds and also deeper into fights. These sorts of athletes usually achieve their KOs through the sheer number / volume of punches thrown and landed. Others achieve their KOs early in rounds and also very early in the fight. For these athletes with frequent early stoppages, you obviously have to be very sharp and also well warmed at the beginning of the fight as early on there is little margin for error. However, with athletes with a tendency toward early KOs if you look at their experiences into the latter rounds, you might find some indication in terms of their stamina and also, when they are no longer dangerous.

Looking further into the opponent's record, you might also want to see whether she/he has ever been stopped before. If there are several fights stopped by RSC and KO, look further into how the opponent was stopped. Doing so will provide you with some indication of physical weaknesses, though maybe also, mental uncertainty. If the athlete has been stopped due to a suspect chin, you know what to go after and by working within your plan to expose your opponent's weakness, you will deplete him of confidence. Few people know their weaknesses better than the athlete, personally.

You might also consider whether the athlete has been knocked down during fights, and then recovered. For example, one of the boxers a client of mine was preparing for held a very high profile. Despite his reputation the boxer was knocked down by several previous adversaries from punches landed to his chin. As such, when we looked closely at the opponent, we found he had adopted a style where he covered up carefully and relied mostly on movement to take him out of harm's way. Every athlete has some useful information that can be gained simply by looking into his record. What I have provided to this point is only the tip of the iceberg.

However, there is also a tendency in boxing to look for greatness, sometimes where greatness does not exist. There are many prospects and contenders in professional boxing with over-inflated records. These sorts of athletes are eventually exposed, though if you look closely into the sections that follow, there are often cracks within their armor long before their records ever show it. It is easy enough to inflate a fighter's record by pairing him/her against weak competition. On the other hand, there are several countries where athletes have weaker records than the standard of their quality. So, look to the numbers in your opponent's record, but remember to look well beyond those numbers to other indicators such as those I provide in this chapter and beyond.

VIDEOS AND YOUTUBE

Beyond the numbers, you need to look very carefully at actual footage from the opponent. In the past, trainers would look high and low for training tapes of the opponent. Many of the best trainers would have a bank of videos to draw on when preparing their boxers. Some of the purpose of that video bank would be directly in relation to a targeted opponent, when footage of the opponent was studied time and again until the coaching staff and then the athlete dissected him down with precision. The other purpose of a video bank was for the coach to educate his boxers in terms of correct and incorrect practices within a fight. In the first case, videos were used to help the client anticipate what was coming in advance, in the second case videos were used for motivational purposes. In both cases, there was no denying the importance of video footage.

First Impressions

Today, it is easy enough to gain the knowledge you need about your opponent and so, how to defeat him/her. We have the worldwide web and with it, YouTube. Most any information about opponents is right there if you know how to look for it, and then, what to look for once you have the footage. When studying all such footage (video and YouTube combined) you need to look at the footage many times before you have the in-depth sense of what you need to know about the opponent. I like to start with a general impression of the opponent. I will just watch the athlete, if possible in his walk from the dressing room right through to ring entry and then, onward through the fight. I typically don't take many notes during that first blink impression of the opponent.

A few years ago there was a book published, titled "Blink". Blink is all about the gut impression we all seem to form at first glance about people and situations. For survival's sake, first blink impressions are virtually invaluable. They are necessary for survival's sake. Consider that if we were to always wait until we processed fully through weather something was threatening or positive, at times we would be swallowed whole by the threats we were attempting to evaluate and make sense of. Blink / first impressions provide us with that gut reaction that needs to inform further research into the strengths and weaknesses of the opponent. So, for your interest, simply take a few notes about your gut reaction about the opponent and then proceed into a deeper look / researching strategy of the opponent.

I will tell you up front that I make most of my living as a high profile sport science researcher. I like to break things down and then put them back together when it comes to research. The objective is to know what I am looking at from its tiniest elements up to the big picture package. The very same analysis is just as important a tool for you as it is for me! Once you have taken that big picture look at the opponent, look further into the components that pull together as parts of the big picture.

So, what sorts of components am I speaking about? If you are an amateur boxer and only have 24 to 48 hours in order to understand your opponent, take a look at what she/he looks like stylistically. Look beyond whether the opponent is an orthodox or southpaw fighter to a few more details such as whether she/he is a fast or slow starter, whether she/he moves only forward and backward, or also laterally. As well, you might wish to consider when the opponent tends to land scoring blows versus when she/he tends to become inactive. Look to whether the boxer can sustain intensity or whether she/he tends to only throw single punches of flurries of punches ongoing throughout the round.

Assuming you are a professional boxer, especially as your record progresses, chances are you will have much more time to scout your opponent. Within the scouting process, look as closely as possible to the sequencing of behaviors from when the opponent is in the dressing room, onward through to the very end of performance. In the dressing room, does the opponent tend to look overwhelmed before bouts, especially those most recent? Look also to whether the corner staff tends to look organized versus disorganized.

Pre-bout Indicators

Next on the agenda, look very closely at what the opponent looks like walking to the ring – assuming you can find that information. For those of you preparing to fight high profile opponents, you should be able to find such footage. Look at the boxer's emotional responses very closely. There are aspects within an athlete's facial expression that cannot be masked, such as micro-expressions. What I mean by micro-expressions are those minor details, especially in the eyes and mouth that suggest the athlete is confident versus self-questioning in those final minutes before the bout. Remember that in the last chapter we spoke about confidence as easy to maintain long before a bout, and much tougher to retain as the athlete comes closer in time to performance. So, look at his/her minute facial expressions and you will gain some small indication of just how confident the athlete really is.

Look beyond the facial expressions to the larger posture of the opponent. Is she/he walking with certainty? Interestingly enough, when I work on basics with my clients, one of the things I zone in on is their posture. I want to see an open and confident posture with shoulders squared, muscles warmed, a regular and rhythmic walking stride, eyes looking ahead toward the ring, with a fully organized corner staff following just behind or just leading the athlete to the ring.

Then, as the boxer steps into the ring, what does he look like then? Is the boxer inactive or staying warm? Is the athlete able to communicate effectively with his corner or is she/he relatively silent and perhaps busy trying to cope with pre-bout jitters? Does he move around the ring before hand or does he stay in his corner? Look to all of these sorts of details and you will understand exactly why he starts the first round the way he does. Remember that each aspect leading up to the bout helps explain the bigger picture why the opponent performs as he does. I recall watching Sergio Martinez warm up for his fights on HBO. In comparison with most of his opponents, Martinez has a relatively active final few minutes in the ring. His activity (to me) has always suggested that he will be sharp in the early rounds. Most recently, that suspicion was confirmed with an early round stoppage of previously undefeated Paul Williams.

The Early Minutes

Next, you need to look at what most every scout would consider, which is how the opponent tends to fight from the first bell. Some boxers are fast starters, where others are much more cautious. There are indeed lots of reasons why boxers are fast or slow starters in performance. Fast starters are sometimes people who are ready to attack, understand the opponent's characteristics well in advance, and bring to the table early confidence. Others are slow starters either out of caution or perhaps due to not being sufficiently warmed immediately before the bout. One thing I know for certain: even the best of pre-bout preparation can be blown just before the bout and in the early seconds of round one. If the opponent tends to let things slide in those final few minutes pre-bout or in the first few seconds of the bout's start, you can start drawing some conclusion in terms of the boxer's organization, discipline, and confidence. On the other hand, if footage indicates that the opponent is well organized, you can anticipate that his skills and capacities will more likely to all be there on the night of performance.

Stealing Rounds

I won't speak about the particulars within each round of the fight, as I am not a boxing coach. I always leave those sorts of things to people with more coaching qualification then me. However, what I do keep a close eye open for is whether the opponent tends to steal rounds through flurries and activity in the last 15 to 20 seconds before the closing bell. Beyond the fact that such athletes are intelligent in their tactics, the strategies they use to steal rounds actually go well beyond the round's closing bell. In addition, by turning the judges' heads in the last few seconds of the previous rounds, they also tend to retain the judges' attention in the beginning few seconds of the next round. So, boxers who tend to steal rounds are savvy and in some cases, their strategies might have benefitted them more than the casual observer would notice.

Global Considerations

More globally, there are minor details that can also tell you something about the opponent. For example, I like to see whether the boxer is a dirty fighter. With one particular opponent I profiled, I noticed that in several fights, he punched after the bell. Knowing that the opponent might do so, I worked with my client's head coach in the final few days before the bout and ensured that all technical sparring and simulation included a component of protecting himself, even after the closing bell to each round. Knowing what I have learned over the years, this sort of insight needs to be engrained into you for a few weeks before the fight, so start pressing in action what you know, soon enough.

Taking a second example, it is useful to know whether the opponent builds in intensity within rounds and from one round to the next, or whether his/her stamina fades. Some athletes are very harmful in the first minutes of the fight and then become relatively harmless, where others become much more dangerous deeper into the fight, with still others proving intense throughout a fight from beginning to end. Look very closely at how the athlete responds as he/she goes deeper into the fight, not only in terms of punch output, but also in terms of emotional expressions. There is an author that I have observed over the years who initially banked quite a bit of success as a high profile professional. In his later fights, I noticed that even in his facial expression he seemed to self-question as he was taken deeper into fights. Some in the media believed his fading was a matter of nutrition and physiology. My view is that physiology sometimes overlaps with psychology. When an athlete lacks confidence in his stamina, he tends to self-question, lose focus, and burn needless energy. Though the end result is the same, athletes with wilting emotional expressions are the sorts of people you ought to take deeper into the later rounds of the fight and then through swarming and aggression, reduce to less than their best.

Finally, few athletes and coaches really take a close look at what happens in the opponent's corner in between rounds. After some years of working with professional boxers I started really becoming systematic. I was somewhat systematic in my approach to working with boxers from the beginning, but when I started working with one boxer in particular things really switched into high gear! As part of that process, at that very moment in time, that client had an opponent as his next bout and the opponent was extremely dangerous, undefeated, and intelligent. When I looked beneath the surface at the YouTube footage however, I began to se weak spots that we could build on and make a strategy around. Looking closely at the athlete when he returned to the corner in one particular bout I noticed that he seemed to shut off and not listen to his head coach. The coach in turn seemed to become frustrated with the athlete, which didn't help the situation. When things went well for the athlete, he would take in the feedback perfectly. Then, if he boxed a sloppy round and got caught, he would shut down in the corner once more.

My belief about that athlete was hit with something profound toward the end of a round he wouldn't absorb the information well when he returned to the corner. Low and behold, when I looked to several fights, I found the very same pattern in the athlete. Though the opponent was top class, he had problems responding to adversity and then rebounding, starting with feedback in the corner after a poor round. So, when the coach and I showed that pattern to our client, who was promising though inexperienced at the top level, he drew his confidence from that weakness. When fight night finally arrived, our predictions were dead on accurate and in the rounds where my client closed, the opponent's corner was less than effective, causing the opponent to start the following round disorganized.

As you can see, when I scout an opponent and profile him, I draw on a lot of YouTube videos. When you look at such footage, my challenge to you is for you to look beneath what others seek and go for the details. Success is built from details and crumbs. Most athletes know that crumbs are important, but few really go after those crumbs relentlessly.

ADDITIONAL INTERNET INFORMATION

Should you have the length of time needed to really investigate your opponent in-depth, move beyond what you can observe through video footage, onward to what the opponent shares through interviews, features, and social networking sites. I have worked with amateur and professional boxers alike and found that most of my clients have loved to speak with the media, as have the opponents of my clients. Though most every athlete given the opportunity likes media exposure, few really understand that what they share can (and should) be resourced to further educate you.

Early On

It is always worthwhile to use a good search engine and Google, Yahoo, or Bing your opponent's name. Even boxers with relatively little experience have information they share in the form of interviews. The best way to proceed is to look at the athlete in relation to his/her most important bouts as case studies. Each bout provides useful information if you look at what the boxer says well I advance of the bout, as the bout approaches, immediately after the bout, and also as the bout fades in to the distance in terms of time lapsed. From interviews well in advance of a bout you will learn what the boxer hopes to do and also what his general confidence level is at that time. What he hopes to do will be indicated as he is asked to explain strategy. Confidence will also be reflected through how he views himself at that point and even how he views his record in relation to previous opponents. Though interview questions vary with each interview and each interviewer, I have found through published research that despite the many differences in interview factors, certain things remain consistent. Those things as far as I am concerned include the boxer's confidence, his/her view of self, and objectives in relation to the next performance.

Near the Bout

As the bout approaches, the boxer might be singing the same tune or perhaps a very different tune. Granted that some of the very best boxers such as Bernard Hopkins are sophisticated in terms of what they let out to the media, even then, you still can gain some important insight about the opponent. So, as the bout draws closer, look and see whether he is till looking for a monumental victory on his part. If the objective changes from monumental performance to trying one's best, there will be indication that confidence is wavering. There might also be indication that the boxer is speaking less about him/herself and more about the opponent. If that is the case, there is the chance that an external focus is being adopted. With a focus on his/her opponent, the athlete will indicate to you that you need to look at several fights for the very same pattern. Sometimes boxers do shift from an internal to an external focus as fights draw near. Those sorts of boxers typically move from a focus of self and the controllables to coping and seeing oneself in relation to a force that they cannot control. On the other hand, the boxer who remains steady and positive as he nears the bout will indicate as such through most every source he has access to, be it interviews or social networking sites.

Immediate Post-bout

The most authentic words spoken by boxers are those immediately post-bout. People have a tendency to think through what they would like to say in public spaces before anything is shared. Right after bouts have been completed, there is no such luxury. I love to listen to Larry Merchant or Max Kellerman interview boxers on HBO and hear what they think of their performances. Winners are either very positive or somewhat positive of their performances. Sometimes winners cannot really explain why they have won a hard fought decision, and in other cases they can. Look to the recent HBO fights of Devon Alexander and Tavoris Cloud (Autumn, 2010), both on the same card. Both, at the end of the card, remained undefeated champions. Immediately post-bout, neither boxer was able to really explain why their wins were so close against opponents they were expected to blow through. In another instance, Jean Pascal one week later was not the least surprised of his win over Chad Dawson, where Chad Dawson externalized accountability to an intentional head butt on the part of Jean Pascal.

The raw emotions of happiness, sadness, confusion, anger, disbelief, and such are authentic / true pictures of where the boxer is at before he makes sense of the bout and explains away some of his performance to patent, well rehearsed responses. Those left in confusion, even after a recent win, start making sense of their experiences at that moment. When immediate post-bout explanations are either unexplainable such as in the case of Arthur Abraham after his loss to Andre Ward, or externalized as in the case of Chad Dawson, the future is often quite promising for their next opponents. Just look carefully at how much accountability your next opponent has taken after his last bout, and also, whether he has engaged in self-exploration, and you will get to the essence of whether he will recover and progress in his next performance. Look more generally at how the opponent typically responds to wins and losses with more and less detail and you can anticipate how systematic he will be against you. There is a lot of information just beneath the surface of immediate post-bout responses. Dig away at the information and you will learn likely more about your opponent's current status than he/she likely knows personally.

Long After the Bout

With distance and time since the last bout, athletes (boxers included) tend to make sense of their last experience. There is a tendency in many boxers to focus inward after a profound success and to focus on the mistakes of those around them, including coaches, officials, opponents and managers, after a recent setback. The challenge, as you likely know from the details outlined in Chapter Seven is to look more globally at why wins were the result and to look internally after a subpar performance.

The reality is that few boxers are able to take an even-handed approach when they dissect their performances. If your opponent appears lopsided in terms of how he explains his/her results, chances are that there was not a thorough debriefing within the days and weeks following recent bouts. Further, with a lopsided / unbalanced understanding of what causes a given performance, your opponent will likely not have a full appreciation of what it takes to be at peak.

If on the other hand your opponent is balanced in understanding the causes just beneath the results, these athletes will know what to integrate in their preparation, systematically. Knowing that your opponent is systematic can only serve to sharpen your focus as you move forward to the bout. There is nothing wring with appreciating the strengths and weaknesses of your next adversary. Knowledge is strength, and from knowledge, you can prepare effectively for the challenges that are before you.

OTHERS IN THE KNOW

There is a tendency to also learn and listen to the experiences of others who have the experiences and knowledge you are seeking to gain. When I go off to training camps with professional boxers, it is always interesting to hear from sparring partners what their experiences have been with a prospective opponent, assuming they hold that experience. Through Facebook as well, you can contact friends and fellow athletes to seek out information about a given athlete. Assuming the sources of information you are contacting are regarded as trustworthy by you and your coach, there can be a wealth of information gained about your opponent though, about unfamiliar venues.

Even when the information you take comes from a creditable source, you need to take it with a grain of salt, so to speak. The experiences of others in the know should be combined with video footage, and also with information available to you and your team on the web. Combined, these sources of information will provide you with the detailed information that you could really build a strategy around.

There is often a tendency in boxers and their working teams to rely solely on one of the aforementioned sources of information when scouting an opponent. Some will tell you that their method is "old school". I respond that you need several sources of information to really inform your decisions and tactics. There is nothing worse then building your strategies for before and during the bout on limited information. I propose that limited information is the end result of either laziness or sloppiness. In either case, the end result is the same: you won't feel fully prepared as the fight draws near.

Your confidence must be built from sound knowledge of yourself, though I argue here, also about your opponent! Go the extra couple of miles and dig deep when seeking out information about your opponent. The knowledge you gain about the opponent will only help you to understand his/her potential tactics and the logic behind those tactics. The reality is that you will notice tactics that are out of the ordinary, that is, unless you saw most of them coming a mile away.

So, the bottom line is to listen to what others have to say about your next opponent, but first, remember that you have to resource only people you trust. The resources you decide to seek out should be more than just trustworthy, they should also be knowledgeable and absolutely, they should have your best interest in mind.

PRESSING YOUR KNOWLEDGE INTO ACTION

Ok, as you can see, I advocate for an in-depth knowledge of your opponent. Obviously, the depth of that information depends on how much time you have to really learn about your opponent. What I mean is that if you only have 24-48 hours to study your opponent, then you need some help to gain what information you can. Start with video and YouTube footage and then add in a few additional sources of information. Do your investigation as early as is possible and not within the final 6-12 hours before the bout. Remember that studying an opponent, is studying, any way you slice it. You will be more likely to remember details you gain as early as possible and then review very briefly in the final few hours leading up to the bout.

Should you have more time to really learn about the opponent, don't let anyone try to tell you to focus simply on video footage. Understanding of another human being is multidimensional. Every opponent brings different tactics to the table. I ask that you learn as much as possible about the opponent, so much so that few things can then take you out of your focus as the bout draws near. Because you have the days available to train in relation to the bout, build the training of your mind systematically in relation to the opponent that is in front of you. Be specific and detailed and you will find that your confidence will be through the roof. Though for some athletes, confidence is a fluffy concept built around guesswork, it will not be the case for you. Your confidence will be built around knowledge, built systematically from facts.

Time tends to slip away very quickly. Never let a day slip by without some additional and deepened understanding of your opponent. You need to understand your target in order to effectively take aim. With all of the available information out there today, there is nothing standing in your way other than the commitment to learning. Though each opponent will bring unique things to the table, through a systematic studying of your opponent, you will gain tremendous skills that you could bring to the table in advance and then during each bout. Excellent boxing careers are built through a detailed approach, and not just from sheer physical talent and solid technical training. I argue that part of your psychological and tactical training must be built in relation to your opponent. Put in the hours before every bout and you will reap successes that will surprise many people. There is nothing better than knowing what will happen in advance so that you could put your best foot forward.

FINAL REFLECTIONS

As we come to the end of this chapter, I want to be very clear at what the logic is behind this chapter. I believe that most of your training and pre-bout preparation has to be built in relation to you. You need to build your strengths and you also need an internal focus. All success begins with you and works outward from that point. I suppose my endorsement of an internal focus is affirmed through the addition of this chapter as Chapter Ten, and not as an earlier addition to the book.

However, you need to understand your opponent, and as you can see, when I speak about understanding the opponent, I really mean it! To really press this chapter into action you need to set aside lots of time – meaning as many days of your mental game as you commit to your physical game. Preparation for each bout is extremely unique, starting with your current status and development. However, when you build your preparation, always do so with a solid understanding of your opponent. Opponents have strengths. In understanding those strengths, you can keep a solid level of confidence, even against the toughest and most complex of adversaries.

SECTION THREE:
IMPLEMENTATION AND REFLECTION

Chapter 11

DEVELOPING YOUR PLAN FOR THE DAY OF THE FIGHT

In boxing, even the best, well-thought out plans and training can be heavily influenced by what happens in the final 24 hours leading up to the performance. I have often watched boxers win and lose their fights within this final essential time, pre-performance. When people talk about plans, the focus is often on what happens "in the fight". In this chapter you are going to see that what happens within the short time leading up to the fight should also be an essential part of your plan.

What follows is my version of a sequencing of events, or pieces, that need to be taken care of in advance of your performance. Some of the pieces are obvious, others might read as logical and basic, and still others might be items you haven't given much thought to. There is little doubt that you are already tackling some of the sections that follow, so if that is the case, this chapter is going to confirm your suspicion – that you are on the right track. Despite the fact that this chapter will be confirming of what you do, chances are there will be crumbs to be picked up from what follows. There are always crumbs to be picked up in every part of your preparation.

In my consulting exposure, I work very closely with athletes and their coaches on this very chapter. In fact, we do much of my work in topics related to this chapter. The objective is always the same: to make the final 24 hours before battle count in a big and positive way!

GENERAL ORIENTATION

To begin with, every athlete has what I like to regard as a general orientation. The general orientation is all about how you are thinking and feeling as the performance draws near. Remember that when we spoke about confidence, it is easy to have a positive general orientation several months, and even several weeks in advance of performance. However, as the performance draws near, meaning in the final days and hours, the acid test of your general orientation can be read and really understood. If there have been unanswered questions that seemed to be let go or overlooked far away from the performance, if they were niggling doubts then, they can mushroom into larger concerns closer to the fight. Conversely, if all of the crumbs have been dealt with all the way along, chances are that your general orientation is pretty good.

Regardless, it is worth knowing and understanding where you are at, as opposed to ignoring gut instincts, especially as performances draw near. Most people rely on gut instincts, which is better than not considering where you are at, entirely. However, I would suggest that a more systematic approach to understanding your general orientation is indeed the way to go! There are several strategies that I have put into practice with competitive boxers over the years. One of the strategies is termed a "stress map". If you use most any search engine and type in the term "stress map", you will find that an assessment tool comes up. It is a basic series of questions in relation to how you are managing life stressors, such as time demands, social connections, work demands, etc. The map should be done probably two to three weeks in advance of your bout. The objective is to identify any nagging concerns that are on your plate well in advance of the performance, and then search for solutions well in advance of the performance. I like to think of this strategy as a sort of clearing of your plate. You need to be clear and focused on only one task at a time, and when you are looking to deliver that great boxing performance, you need to focus entirely on boxing and what needs to happen in the ring.

Within the final week in advance of the performance, the objective is to have cleared your schedule so that all that is on your mind is boxing. No doubt there will be other life demands that you will need to take care of, but those sorts of things can mostly be done without stress. What I mean is that the really pressing and lingering tasks in your life need to be freed from your schedule by fight week. Only then can you really perform up the potential that we are really looking for within this book.

Far too often, boxers are so overwhelmed with the compounded tasks on their plate in the week before the fight that they give up part of their edge, unnecessarily. You need to keep your edge and count on the fact that your opponent will not be as detailed and organized as you are. Be the sort of detailed athlete who clears your plate the week of the fight, so that you can pave the way to excellence.

Next, It becomes your head coach or your sport psychology consultant's tasks to gain a reading on you within that final week, leading up to performance. What sorts of things should you gain a reading on? There are four items I have learned through my working team. You need to consider your (1) physical preparation / technical preparation, (2) tactical preparation, (3) psychological preparation, and (4) general orientation. Each item obviously holds its own part to the whole of your general orientation, meaning how you feel in those final few days. Physical / technical preparation is all about how you trained for the fight. Did you train hard and with the correct intensity to withstand the physical demands needed to excel at the level you are about to compete at? Next, did you train specifically in relation to the level of your opponent, and also based on a good, solid understanding of your opponent'(s) style(s)? Are you mentally focused and organized in relation to this fight? Finally, How do you feel generally – that gut feeling? Each of these questions should be asked of you in the evening before you go to sleep, or at the very end of a day's training in that final week pre-bout. You need to consider each question carefully and assign a number from 0-10. Your coach should record your scores each day and use these after the bout to help you make sense of your performance result. The final time the scores should be asked of you is about 15 minutes before you walk to the ring in fight night.

Now, the objective is to gain a very clear understanding of where you are at in that final week of training and pre-performance preparation. To gain that ever important understanding though, you need to be perfectly honest with yourself and your team. The objective is to come as close to 10 as possible by the final night, before you step into the ring and excel. Typically, if there is a score that is really low, it shows as really low early in the week. If that is the case, you have lots of time to build up your numbers.

Engaging in the four part questions each night brings you and your team onto the same page. You need to communicate with your team, and you all need to understand where you are at each day. I have seen some athletes unravel before important performances and more often than not, their undoing happens several days before the fight – it's just that no one noticed, and the athlete didn't communicate the concern(s). It is time to be open with your team and to trust them with an honest answer to all of the four questions. The objective also, is to have the best score, as you get closer to the fight. When readings are off a little, then it is time to speak with your team and see what refinements need to happen, and then to make them happen.

SETTING THE TONE THROUGH REST AND MENTAL FOCUS

Mental focus and rest work hand in hand, meaning that they work together. It is only possible to think clearly when you are well rested. Without rest, your mind will not be as sharp as it needs to be, for the right aspects of you to surface at the right time. If you are performing late at night, in the final few days before the bout, you should likely go to sleep a little bit later in the evening, but also regain those hours in the following morning. Some people need eight hours of sleep, and others need ten hours. The thing about sleep is that it works the very same way as a bank account – it works by compound interest. If you invest the correct amount of sleep in the days leading up to your performance, or if you are in a tournament, also throughout the tournament's days, then you will remain well rested and sharp. If on the other hand, if you cut an hour here and an hour there, before you know it you will lose your sharpness. By the time you realize that you are tired, it will be too little, too late as you look to rest just before the performance.

I recall some years ago I traveled with a national boxing team to a Pan American Games. One of their star athletes happened to also be a very engaged client of mine. The boxer was cutting sleep each night as he went out to meet other athletes in the Village where all the athletes and their staff lived. I remember sharing my observation with the athlete well in advance of the first day of bouts and he wasn't much interest in banking sleep. Before long, he was eliminated from the tournament prematurely, to a weaker fighter. My guess is that the weaker fighter was also the more rested fighter, and so the clearer thinker when things counted most. See what I mean by losing great preparation in those final few days and hours?

Rest means much more than just banking sleep. It also means using your time wisely in that final week. Some years ago, I worked with a very promising professional boxer as he prepared for a critical world title bout. The boxer had all kinds of things scheduled for the week of the fight. He and his team (me included) were literally running for several days early in the week, fight week. We spent countless hours in the car, and because the coach and I are very details oriented, we sat down with the entire team and tried to simply tasks and delegate out the running around that didn't need to involve the working team. Because we also had an open-minded athlete to work with, the team regrouped and the athlete became a world champion.

The lesson to be learned from the story directly above is that athletes and their teams sometimes give up lots of energy by trying to do "everything" on their own, and not farming out tasks that need to be handed over to someone else who is trustworthy. Rest happens through organizing your day and making good decisions that simplify your life. That week leading up to the fight will be filled with lots of opportunities to either make good choices or energy depleting choices. Much like sleep, you have to bank good decisions and before you know it, fight night will be there, and you will be sharp, and so, ready to do your thing.

EATING RIGHT

You might not have guessed it, but what you eat also can alter how you think and how you feel. When you over-eat, I will bet that you feel extremely sluggish and slow thinking. There are certain foods that sit very heavy in your stomach and tend to slow you down, literally. Other foods are high-energy foods that are much more easily digestible. When you eat the right foods, assuming you are tuned into your body, you should feel sharp, charged with energy, and ready to take on the challenges of the day. Food is one of those profound and also under-rated aspects that fewer boxers consider than you could imagine.

I have watched many a developing elite boxer initially under-estimate the importance of food. At the beginning some athletes stuff themselves full of processed foods, eat lots of greasy meals, and cheat with diets that actually take away from their true potential as athletes. When athletes are in their late teenage years and early twenties, some don't give enough thought to self-care and in this case, the aspect of eating right.

Slowly, the more adaptive, intelligent athletes modify their ways and learn what foods sit right for them. The importance of eating to thinking is so profound that few really give what they eat the focus it deserves. Several years ago I worked with a very promising middleweight boxer who tended to eat junk food all the time. As he grew older, he struggled more with making weight the week of the fight. He would land up dehydrating himself to the point where he was virtually exhausted. Before long, the boxer was no longer a middleweight and so he moved up to super middleweight. Shortly afterward he ballooned out further and became a light heavyweight. Unfortunately for that extraordinary athlete, because he was fighting several divisions above where he should have been, he ended boxing against much stronger opponents and he eventually lost his confidence and now he is little more than an average boxer.

When you choose to eat meals, choose the correct ones. Make what you eat a habit so that when you arrive at the final few days before the fight, it becomes much easier to drop those last few pounds and ounces. When you manage what you eat, life becomes much easier and you are able to focus on the task at hand, meaning your performance, and not your weight.

Focusing more on the topic of this chapter, what you eat also has a direct influence on how you feel on fight day. If you have a rumbling – upset stomach after eating something that doesn't agree with you, then your focus is on you, but not on your boxing performance. There are performance foods that provide you with energy when you need them most. In the working team that I am a part of, athlete dietary intake is an evolving process. There are things to eat directly after the boxer makes weight, things to eat the morning of the fight, and things to eat and drink throughout the day, even in the dressing room a few hours before the bout. Every boxer needs to look very closely at what they eat, when they eat it, whether the food agrees with them, truly, and what its benefits are to performance. The bottom line is performance and every food choice you make should take you to better performance, through better long-term energy. What you choose to like has to be a matter of what benefits you most in performance. Though it is sometimes cool and even funny to challenge this sort of common sense by eating junk and performing despite what you eat, rest assured that what you eat eventually catches up with you – you are what you eat! Make your food choices count so that your body is free to follow and sometimes also lead your mind.

THE MORNING BRIEFING

On the morning of the fight, there are always a few things that need to happen. Depending on your circumstance, you might need to weigh-in, and you will definitely need to have your breakfast. Once you have done these tasks, it will be time to sit down and meet with your working team, to visit or re-visit the performance plan. Sometimes coaches and athletes meet over breakfast to engage in a morning briefing. I used to support such a strategy, however now I like to have athlete and coach schedule in a very relaxed breakfast, and also a relaxed lunch and dinner on fight day. Every meal counts nutritionally and I would bet that it counts most when you could digest it. Have you ever tried to eat a meal while trying to talk to people about performance related topics? In my experience all that ever results from such initiatives is indigestion and an incomplete conversation where people are trying to focus on two things at once – eating and the conversation topic.

Briefings are important and they need your undisturbed – full attention. When you enter into a briefing, you need to shit down your cell phone, wireless device, computer, telephone, and also place a "do not disturb" sign on your room door. When people arrive at the door other than those needed for the briefing session, they need to be turned away or ignored. The working team that is focused in the fight needs to first focus before the fight, on the fight! The boxer and coach who cannot engage in a focused conversation before the fight will be setting the tone for an unfocused performance in the fight. Remember that you cannot expect more under pressure than what you do as a practice without pressure. Pressure magnified habits and those habits can bring out the best and the worst in each of us.

So, now that we have set the tone for the meeting, briefings should be very short and extremely focused. Athletes and coaches are getting nearer to performance and there is sometimes some edginess / irritability that goes along with those final hours of lead up time. So, meetings need to be used as a sort of touching base and an opportunity to push people closer to focus, and not to drain energy unnecessarily. When sitting down, do so at a good time in the morning, several hours before the fight. For coaches, have your specific reminder points on hand for the discussion, but have the athlete lead the discussion. If you are the boxer, lead the discussion, just like you will lead the fight. Describe what your plan is for the fight and the very specific and simple plan that you will follow for your departure, warm-up, walk to the ring and most importantly, once the bell goes.

In total, the briefing meeting should be no more than 20-25 minutes. To use your time wisely, be prepared for the meeting with an agenda, and a list of items to be discussed. As the boxer, be prepared with details and also any questions or concerns that you need to bring to the table. Remember that communication has to be honest and fully transparent. If you are the coach, be prepared to identify any points your athlete has overlooked and use the meeting to ensure that the day and your athlete are on track. By connecting in the morning, everyone remains on the same page. Moving beyond maintenance, those last countdown hours before the fight are times when the team has to pull tighter together. The morning briefing is one opportunity that ensures you are all moving in the correct – same direction.

STAYING LIMBER

Several hours before the fight, it is always my suggestion that boxers stretch their legs and go for a walk. I have arrived at this belief having watched many amateur elite boxers stay in their room and sleep the day away before they fight. When the athletes finally wake up, they are sluggish and in fact, over-rested. Your body needs to be extremely sharp to perform at its best. Rest is an important aspect of what makes you sharp, and I have suggested some important reference points a few sections above this one. However, like most things, rest has to be part of bout day, and not the exclusive focus. Don't just sleep the entire day away and expect your body to be awake at the right moment.

Going for a walk is so important to your performance that you might not have fully realized just how significant it is. The walk helps you get out of your room, fill your lungs with fresh air, and clear your mind. As you get your heart up a little just by walking, your body will wake up a little and your blood will start flowing. Though you don't really need to structure your thinking about the bout a few hours ahead, let your mind travel through the important pieces of your strategy, confirmed earlier in the day from the morning briefing session. Thinking about the strategies will serve as touch stones of what you need to do, sort of like a short review of what you are looking to do in the fight.

The question is should you walk alone or go with a friend? Either option is perfectly acceptable, depending on your preference. If you choose to walk alone, the walk will serve as a time to focus inward, gather your strengths, and do that last minute mental hardening that needs to take place before exceptional performance. Should you choose to walk with a buddy or coach, that strategy is also perfectly fine. Your walking buddy needs to be supportive of you and so, the relaxed discussion and thinking that happens on the walk should be about brief reminders. You need to lead the discussion and the person you walk with should not pull away from the energy and focus that you need to keep inside of yourself.

Walks always vary in time and from what I have found, they can last from 20-45 minutes. Shorter periods of time don't permit enough time for you to stretch your legs, think inside of yourself, and have your blood flowing effectively. Longer walks to me are overkill because you have to save your energy and your legs for the fight ahead. Remember, much like all other aspects on performance day, everything in moderation.

PACKING

Though I have spoken in earlier sections about the importance of being organized, I cannot emphasize enough the importance of organization. Having traveled for several years with national teams, I am always puzzled when athletes forget things only to realize that an important piece of equipment is missing when they need it most. I have witnessed boxers arriving at the venue just before they fought at huge international tournaments, where they were missing their head gear, mouth pieces, shoes, shorts, socks, warm-up music, and even their entire equipment bag!

How is it possible that someone could be so sloppy and disorganized in their final efforts? As I have pointed out to you at the very start of this chapter, great training and preparation can be completely undone in those final few hours before your performance, and forgetting to pack and then bring your equipment with you to the venue is a prime example. Every athlete I work with is required to have a detailed – precise packing list. We commit to perfect organization. There is nothing better than knowing that you have everything you need at your fingertips as you traveling from your hotel to the competition site. On the other hand, there is nothing worse that traveling to the site, all the while wondering whether you have everything you need. Performance is all about removing the questions marks and freeing your mind and body for performance.

You need to develop your packing list at least a week before you leave town for your performance(s). When you initially write down what you need, you will find that you are missing a few things, and so your list might refine. By the end you should have a formal list of equipment that includes what you will wear from head to toe, what you need for your warm-up, and also what you need for after the fight. Think chronologically from what is needed from when you walk into the competition site to when you return to your hotel.

Next, what you need to do is paste the packing list to the inside of your equipment bag. When it is time to pack, you need to empty all of the items from the equipment bag onto your bed. Even though you likely have packed the bag several days earlier, empty it on the bed so that nothing is lost and then, as you put each item into the bag, place a check mark beside that item on the packing list. By the end of the packing process each item must be "checked off" on your list. Doing so will confirm to you that everything you need is in the bag and ready to go.

As an aside, you need to pack your own equipment and not leave that task to anyone else. You are accountable and in control of your equipment, this task of packing is not one to assign to a team member. Not long ago I witnessed a high profile client having one of his support staff packing his bag. That procedure was corrected immediately and even with a client at the every pinnacle of his boxing career, I insist that he does his own packing. The reason why is that nothing should ever be left to chance, not literally, and definitely not in the mind of the boxer.

Finally, it is great to pack your equipment perfectly. The final step to close the loop is for you to bring your equipment bag with you from departure to arrival at the competition site. I have seen bags lost every step along the way, from boxers leaving them in hotel rooms, to leaving them in taxis and buses. That bag should be in your hand as you leave your hotel room and it is should stay on your lap until you step out of your transportation to the venue. Then, as you step out of the vehicle, the bag should be in your hands once more until it is set down at the exact location where you will be warming up. To conclude the process, the bag should never be let out of the eyesight of a team member once it is set down.

BEING PUNCTUAL ON ARRIVAL

With the best of pre-bout organization to the point of arrival, still, things need to stay organized even in the final stage of departure to the competition site through the moment that you step foot in the arena – building. You might be one of those punctual athletes who organizes yourself extremely well where you keep to the schedule for fight night. If you are one of those people, your habits will place you ahead of many of your opponents.

There are boxers who shift away from their plans by either getting antsy and then leaving to the arena much too early. If you are like to be at the arena early, the decision is yours to make. Just make certain that you bring some food, music, and all of the necessary equipment items to keep you occupied so that time passes quickly. So, there is nothing really wrong with arriving early at the venue, but decide on that plan in advance of departure and have your working team also endorse the plan so that you all stay on the same page. Remember, stick to the plan and by doing so, stay on the same page with the people who are going to support your performance that night.

On the other hand, there are people who always run late. Typically, late people know that they are late and they have built their lives around being late. Late people are late to airports, meetings, and also, to their pre-fight preparation. I have witnessed coaches and sport science staff pulling their hair out when a boxer or staff member once again runs late. Fight night is a time where people need to be at their clearest and most organized. And yet, by running late, the person who is the culprit has thrown a monkey wrench into what needed to be a systematic preparation. With the working team now trying to get back on their track, the members enter into coping mode where they have to respond to disorganization. With stress levels going up within the working team, people are no longer at their sharpest. Performance preparation is a proactive exercise and not a reactive exercise. My challenge to you is for you to stay with the plan and in so doing, support an organized approach to performance.

I will say that I have worked with organized and disorganized members in the various working teams I have experienced. At the disorganized end of the continuum, I recall one athlete who was almost an hour late in his departure to a bout where he was defending a world title! At the other end of the continuum, I work with a head coach (Marc Ramsay) and a cut man and assistant coach (Russ Anber), both of whom are meticulously organized people. Given the choice between the two strategies, I choose organization every time. Even the most knowledgeable and capable of teams under-perform when they encounter or create disorganization.

SCOUTING AND GENERAL ONSITE ADAPTATION

The performance arena is the physical environment where your performance begins to unfold as you've planned it. I am a big believer in scouting the arena several days in advance of performance day so that you can get a good feel of what the arena will be like on fight day.

I agree that you won't have a full sense of what it will feel like filled with people, lights, officials, athletes, etc. However, you begin to have a sense of what the environment will be like and all that you need to do is complete the missing parts of the picture with your imagination. Take a close look at your warm-up area and then walk from that area directly to where the ring will be placed. Know the physical pathway from the warm-up area to where you will be going.

As related to pre-performance preparation, I always encourage my athletes to drop their things off in their dressing room and to take a few minutes and have another look at the performance arena. This time it will be much closer as an environment to the one you will be performing in shortly. Stay in the corner of the arena, have a look around, notice the environment in the arena, and then take 4-5 deep breaths and relax. This environment is yours to take control of. Remember, by controlling yourself, you will slowly take control of your opponent, the referee, the judges, the audience, and in short, the entire environment.

As I shared with you in Chapter Eight when we spoke about adaptation, you need to adjust effectively to your environment. The arena is now your environment and so you have to impose control by staying within your plan. Step one, drop off your equipment in the room, step two, scout the arena for 4-5 minutes, step three, return to your warm-up and move deeper into your plan.

THE ROOM LIST

When consulting as part of a working team, one of the focal points in our discussion has always been on dressing room structure. Part of that structure is about the "who" – meaning who gains access to the athlete and the warm-up environment. As you can appreciate, there are certain people who are good friends that away from performance night, are great to hang out with. There are other people aside from when you are doing performance related tasks that you would never hang out with. When it comes to dressing room or warm-up area lists, the choices you make of who gains access should be about friendship as much as what benefits you and your team's focus and concentration.

I will say that I have seen all kinds of different ideas from athletes and staff of who should be found within the warm-up area. Boxing is a social sport and boxers train in facilities where they develop lots of friendships. As the boxers gain in experience and credibility, their web of friendships and supporters widens to the point where there are lots of sponsors, managers, media, friends, and family, beyond members of the working team. When all of the above groups of people become part of the warm-up area, they enter to support you, the athlete! They want to wish you the best, shake your hand, hug, and basically let you know that they are behind you. I love this social aspect of boxing, very much. It is what keeps me in the sport – the environment is always amazing and supportive.

When it comes to a question of who should be in the warm-up area though, you need to think in terms of end objective. What really needs to happen in the final 120 minutes before you walk to the ring? From what I know, grounded in some experience, is that athletes need to focus inward on themselves. The focus inward formally starts about 24 hours before the performance when for the professional athlete, there is a meal with team and maybe some select friends. On fight day, the athlete has less people in contact with him/her and as a result, there is lots of time for the boxer to focus inward on what needs to be done in the performance ahead. Shifting now to you, as you step into the venue, your focus needs to continue to narrow because ultimately when you step into the ring, it is you who engages in the battle and you do that alone, with some help for your corner in between rounds. So, the process of narrowing has to take on that narrowing structure where, as the warm-up proceeds, you need to have a structured environment that facilitates that narrowing of your concentration.

In the past, I remember working with a well-known world champion whose coach asked me if a reporter could shadow me in the dressing room as I supported the athlete and monitored the room during the athlete's warm-up. My immediate gut feeling was that we didn't need an extra body in the room during this critical time in the athlete's preparation. Further, I felt that the focus should be on the athlete and what is best for him, not my own personal exposure. When I entered the dressing room that evening, it was filled with 30-40 people all supporting and cheering for the athlete as he went deeper into his warm-up. These cheerleaders believed that they were building motivation in the athlete and also affirming their support of the athlete. I watched the athlete grow increasingly fatigued as the night went on. When the time to perform came, the athlete started well and then faded in the later rounds. He won the fight as unanimous decision, but in the process he also was stopped in the final minutes.

My view is that less is more when it comes to who gains access to a dressing room. Only the working team, meaning the people who've been consistent forces in the athlete's bout preparation should be in attendance. The decision to have a tight working group around the athlete allows her/him to focus inward. Working team members know not to draw away from the boxer's concentration and so, they allow an inward focus to happen when it needs to happen in those final few hours. Be very picky about who is identified and written onto your list and also, develop your list of people with your head coach before fight night. Then, go the next step and ensure that a member of your working team monitors who gains access. That person will look after your interests and allow you to clear your mind so that the focus is performance.

THE TUNE-UP

In relation to the tuning up process, let me be clear, I am not a coach, so I will not speak about technical aspects. However, I will say that what needs to be achieved in a bout tune-up is somewhat different from your general warm-up. Though some of the structure might be very similar such as stretching, skipping rope, and shadow boxing, just before you perform, the details of pad work need to reflect the strategy for the fight. I have observed that the best of coaches and athletes use pad work as a form of review of what is planned for the ring. Athletes and coaches who warm-up generally with conventional tactics that don't vary by opponent, really aren't tuning-up for the bout ahead. By being very specific in pad work, you have an opportunity to reinforce the tactics in terms of punches, footwork, body positioning, speed, and coordination. The psychological benefit of engaging in a specific tune-up allows you to build further focus on what is ahead within the performance.

Boxers vary in terms of what they need within their pad work in relation to intensity. Some like to work consistently and intensely, especially as they come closer in time to departure to the ring. Others like to practice their pads in spurts. The decision of what works best for you is one that you finalize with your coach, always with the end focus of breaking a very good sweat so that you are ready to go by the time the tune-up is completed.

Toward the end of the tune-up there should be a few minutes left over for final reminders and an exchange of communication between you and your head coach. Remember that as you prepare to walk to the ring, you aren't doing so alone. You have a corner that will be working with you, and for you! Stay within your team and keep the lines of communication open, always. I have seen some athletes grow progressively silent as they come to the end of their tune-ups – which is fine. However, always remember that you are the center of your team and that at very least, you need to listen (and hear) what your coach has to say. The pattern of listening carefully starts in training, continues during the tune-up, and sustains from the moment you step into the ring, onward to the final bell and your victory.

WALKING TO THE RING

The walk to the ring is an important next step in the move towards performance. If you look at Mike Tyson's walks to the ring when he was at his best, man was he focused! Tyson was an athlete who was really narrow and in the moment. He didn't see the crowd, and as he made his way to the ring, his eyes were locked onto the ring and then onto the opponent. Walks tell me a significant amount about whether the boxer is ready to perform, or not. Eyes need to be steady and the boxer needs to keep his/her tune-up progressing forward by keeping the heart rate elevated. Far too often, walks take away from tune-ups and by the time the boxers get to the ring, they're cold and flat-footed.

Ask yourself what you would like to achieve in your walk to the ring and how you can use the walk to build your momentum and positive energy. Focus inward, keep your eyes focused on the ring and keep moving aggressively toward the ring. The objective is to stay warm, but also at the same time about making that important first impression with the judges and ring official. People have a tendency to think and work subjectively. Judges and officials are biased, for better and for worse. You need to be focused for your own benefit and in so doing, you will gain the focus of the judges, the audience and shortly afterward, also the opponent.

So, the walk has to be in part about your posture. You need to be imposing and in being, you will appear imposing to observers, also. Posture is one of those things that count as a double dividend. There are gains to you directly. By opening your posture you will automatically build your confidence. When people slouch their shoulders, they make themselves smaller. As they become smaller they also become subordinate much like any animal without confidence shrinks in the face of adversity. You need to do the very opposite and make yourself larger than life! Open your shoulders, look ahead, walk with conviction and you will find that your confidence will soar to great heights. Guess what, the double divided will happen when others gain the very same insight about you. IN doing for yourself directly, you will also look imposing to others, including the officials and your opponent.

Then, as you step into the ring, you need to take a deep breath. The objective is for you to build your focus and for that to happen, you need oxygen to your brain. Then, open up your shoulders and look to the crowd. That's right, take a second and look at the environment for just one second if you like. Then, walk around the ring, acknowledge the referee, and then move back to your corner and lock eyes with the opponent. He is now your target and he is in your sight.

STAYING WARM, STAYING SHARP

Not long ago, I traveled overseas with a professional boxer as he fought for a world title. The athlete is an amazing person, bright, athletic, the sort of person I really respect. He is one of those sorts of people who is detail oriented, meaning he is a really good student of the sport. In those final few minutes before his performance, I watched as this long drawn out ceremony went on. I hoped that the moments following the ceremony would be great ones for the athlete – he deserved success.

At the end of the night, my client lost a hard fought decision by one point on two judges' scorecards to his opponent, in the opponent's city. Win and lose, it is the job of the athlete and working team to always dissect the performance after the fact, learn what works, identify what doesn't work, and then to integrate those lessons systematically from that point onward. After the fight, a critical piece of information identified by the athlete as that he was a little cold at the start of the fight. In hindsight, he lost some of the benefits of his tune-up in those final few minutes in the ring just before the first bell. As I have told you all along, performances are won and lost on even small decisions, especially as the bout is about to happen.

Contrasted with the story above, I watched Sergio Martinez prepare for a recent bout where again, a long ceremony went on just before the bout. His head coach used his palms and was engaging in some pad work to keep Martinez focused and warm. When the first bell chimed Martinez was sharp and ready for what would follow. Martinez in my eyes is one of those special boxers, not only because he is fast, but from my standpoint, especially because he is disciplined and professional. Martinez and his staff were undoubtedly very well aware that they could benefit from the long drawn out ceremony to build focus while the other athlete did what even the best boxers sometimes do and coast.

With all of the minor ceremonious aspects out of the way, the next step in the process is to touch gloves. This next progression forward in the final minutes pre-bout is another area where you can score a double dividend. You will walk forward to the center of the ring, along with your coach. As you step forward you need to remember many of the details needed in your walk to the ring. You need to be open and large in your posture and your eyes have to be locked straight in front of you onto the target: your opponent. As you arrive at center ring your eyes need to be steady. To contrast what I am proposing think of athletes who step to center ring and shift around, all the while looking away from their opponent. More often than not, those athletes see themselves as weaker. They also give away their confidence to the boxer who stands in front of them! You need to remember that in being physically confident and right there, you will feel in control and also, your opponent is also going to feel your presence.

FINAL REFLECTIONS

Well, lots of things to consider when it comes to developing your plan. Some might tell you that you can over plan and that simpler plans are always better. In part, I would agree with that statement. Simple plans are always best. I would add to the above that commonsense contributes to the development of a simple, but effective plan. You need to look closely at the aspects that need to be developed into your plan and be very precise about what you are doing, and also where you might be a little thin in terms of substance.

Plans don't happen all at once. They happen a little bit at a time and they are built and refined over years. Rest assured that Sergio Martinez, Bernard Hopkins, and other very organized high-end fighters have extremely well developed, evolved plans. Even their plans continue to refine and build with each fight, as the athletes continue to learn about what they need to do to be at their very best.

You need to chip away at this chapter before, though also after each fight so that you can also build a solid plan for the final 24 hours before you perform. Remember that often, fights are won and lost in those final few hours. My hope is that you will capitalize on the final 24 hours pre-bout and in so doing, rise to the occasion while your opponent does what many developing athletes do and take a middle of the road approach to their preparation, within only moderate planning.

Plans need to happen well in advance of the fight and they need to be developed collaboratively. You need to work hand in hand with your head coach and working team, with all of you contributing to its development and refinement. Cover off all of the bases! Once that plan is agreed upon, the commitment must shift to pressing the plan into action. A former mentor once told me that: "if you fail to plan, you plan to fail". As you could see from this chapter alone, I agree with those words and endorse them with my own clients.

Chapter 12

FIGHTING YOUR FIGHT

Finally, we now turn to performance psychology for the fight itself. By the time you arrive at the moment to perform, a considerable amount of preparation has been invested into your preparation and mental readiness. With all of the groundwork already under your belt, more often than not, the performance should simply come forward and reflect your extensive commitment and hard work. I always think of competition as the magnifying glass that exposes all that you have done in advance of the performance, for better and for worse. If you've eaten well all along, you likely had no problem making weight and now, you have all of the energy in the world. If you trained with focus, than focus is exactly the habit that should reveal itself throughout your performance. If you have planned well leading up to the fight and then stuck to your plan, than you will have very few nagging question marks as you step to center ring and touch gloves. What you are now is a direct reflection of the many decisions you've made all the way along in your preparation. At a certain point there is no hiding the truth!

In this chapter, the goal is to discuss how to finalize all of the hard work you've done to this point. Remember how I told you earlier that your good decisions were investments in you? Now it is time to cash in on your hard work, but even in the moment of performance, there are a few touchstones that you need to remember and exploit. Boxers win and lose based on the decisions they make all the way along in their preparation, including those identified in the performance. It's time to unmask your thorough preparation and bring all of your hard work to reality in the form of excellence.

CLEARING YOUR MIND AND LETTING GO

Some years ago, I wrote a book about performance psychology for an entirely different sport. I was competing at the international level at that time and found in my own experiences and also in the observations of the others around me that few were the athletes who took a "leap of faith". You need to take a leap of faith in your performance and trust that your preparation was comprehensive and well though out. With all of that hard work banked, you need to let go and be you.

However, trust in self, team and bout preparation is something that many athletes do not fully give themselves up to. I have heard many a coach speak of the most talented athletes who do not deliver greatness on the day as backyard performers. To some extent I understand what these coaches mean – some athletes, even with the best of preparation, never nail down a good performance when the opportunity is right there within their grasp. From my background in the mental side of sport science, I explain backyard performances as the result of limited resilience or limited confidence.

The reality is that athletes don't just naturally have more or less confidence at their core. Athletes are developed and refined carefully, with their training building the hardening of the skin that is really necessary for great performances to be delivered when they're needed most. As a Canadian boxing enthusiast, I never really understood what hardening was until I worked with a former national team coach from Cuba, Pedro Diaz. Pedro hardens his athletes in a way that allows me to walk in, help athletes organize their thinking, and then with our combined efforts, the boxer is able to let go, trust himself and his team. The athletes we work with at very least most of the time, approach their fights with enthusiasm, and then their moment comes, they let what they have leaned surface to the very top.

The thing about letting go, is that for you to do so, you first need to do all of the necessary spade work in your preparation where all question marks, meaning concerns, are addressed as they happen. With a comprehensive approach and no question marks, you can let go. On the other hand, if you carry a number of unresolved questions on your shoulders leading up to the fight and the questions remain untouched, your performance will be weighed down with concerns, caution, guessing, and inhibition.

In the immediate performance, the person with unresolved questions will become weighed down by those concerns. Over time, such athletes learn to lower their standard and cope with hardship instead of letting go and allowing greatness to surface. In every boxer is the relative opportunity for greatness. Greatness is all about decisions banked leading up to each fight, and also, banked from one fight preparation and result to the next in a form of history.

The thing you need to remember is to make the right decisions in each fight, and the dividends will be gained in small amounts within each fight, but the better performances in each fight will then allow you to shoot for larger performances as you move deeper into your boxing, from one performance to the next. Only then can you touch gloves, be at peace with yourself, and then allow yourself the opportunity to perform without boundaries and inhibitions.

THE FEELING OUT PROCESS

The feeling out process happens once the first bell has rung and the performance begins for real. In the amateur ranks, I have noticed that the most confident athletes usually feel out their opponents very quickly. Within the first 30-45 seconds, some of my clients were able to size up some formidable opponents and then move forward, start implementing their plans, and slowly begin taking control of their opponents, the judges, the audience, and in essence, the entire performance venue. Obviously, when I have worked with professional athletes deeper into their careers, there was much more time to feel out opponents though even then, some were extremely quick in formalizing their plans and taking it to the opponent.

The feeling out process to me is very interesting. The wise boxer uses his opportunity in the first minute or so of the first round to scout his opponent and draw some very useful conclusions. Those conclusions would include where the opponent is weak in his defense, how confident the opponent is, how he moves in terms of reflexes and linear and lateral movement, and also the most general sense of what the opponent is all about. Even when boxers have extensive scouting reports and psychological profiles of their opponents, until they are actually in the ring with the opponent, they don't have a true sense of what their opponents are really about. Some opponents are faster than anticipated and others are slower. Some are far tougher to touch than video footage might have led even the well-prepared boxer to believe. Scouting provides you with that first blink impression of exactly what is in front of you and so, what needs to happen for you to work your plan.

In Chapter Eight I spoke a considerable amount about what you need to do in order to adapt and then perform at your best. The scouting out process personifies the adaptation process. The objective when scouting is to experiment and see what really works, what might not work, and then to refine your performance plan accordingly and move forward onto excellence. Embrace the scouting time and use it to your best advantage. Remember that the best plans are built around knowledge and not around speculation. Move beyond guess work and really get to the very heart of what within your skills should be pressed into action.

As the scouting process comes to an end, I have noticed within boxers that those who were thorough all of a sudden seem to have a sense of what needs to be done, and then they almost smile when it registers that they have the opponent's number. If you are thorough in your scouting, you will have your opponent's number and when you gain that realization, he will see it in your eyes. Gaining that sense of how to expose your opponent's weakness will then become another one of those double dividends where you gain benefits in terms of knowledge about the opponent and just afterward, your opponent will see in your eyes that you have the insights to expose him.

CLOSING EACH ROUND

Some years ago one of my clients was fighting at Foxwoods Resort and Casino again the late great Vinnie Paz. At the time I did not fully understand the level of accomplishments achieved by Paz though more recently I better understand just how good he was. I recall watching the fight from the sidelines. My client was boxing well for much of each round and I noticed a pattern where Paz increased his intensity in the final 20 seconds or so at the end of every round. Some in the audience were using the term "stealing rounds" in relation to the performance.

Today, I recognize the genius though also the simplicity of Paz' strategy. When judges decide to score their rounds, they do so in relation to the round as a whole. And yet, if you listen to television coverage, even the coverage provided by the most creditable of commentators, they sometimes say that an athlete who was relatively inactive throughout a round won it in the final seconds. Judges obviously vary in quality in both the amateur and professional ranks, but even the most experienced judges sometimes rule in favor of an athlete who was most active toward the end of the round.

In the amateur ranks these days they score point and not rounds. Granted you might think that this point is lost on me based on what I have said so far, but hear me out. A boxer in the amateurs might be ahead on the scorecards and even stay ahead within a given round despite the fact that the other boxer surges toward the end of the round. However, there is a phenomenon in social psychology called a "recency effect". When there is a short lag time in between the performance and the next stage of the performance, it seems that judges' eyes gravitate toward the boxer who held their attention just before the end of the round. As the next round begins, the judges' eyes are then drawn to the busier fighter in terms of the more likely person to land the scoring blows. And so, not only did the boxer who closed the round actually "close the round". He also has earned the judges' eyes for the beginning of the next round. Thirty seconds here, thirty seconds there and all of a sudden the intelligent fighter has not only stolen a point or two. The intelligence of the fighter in recognizing the biases of judges has allowed him to win much more easily than he would have otherwise.

At the professional level, the recency effect comes into play much more actively. Rounds are decided often based on a general picture of what transpired in the round. When judges decide who gets the 10 versus the 9, that decision is made quickly at the end of the round. I wonder psychologically what information comes to their minds most readily? If one were to buy into the recency effect, then judges likely recall what they witnessed most recently before they record down their scores. And so, Vinnie Paz was dead on the money when he chose as his strategy for that fight to raise his intensity in the dying seconds of each round.

Though I do not guarantee the professional boxer that closing the round will assure him/her the edge at the end of the round, I do like the odds in favor of such a ruling. You need to fight your fight: there is no denying that point. Over and above that strategy, my suggestion is that you be the one with the most to say in those final 20-30 seconds before the round ends. If you could then begin the next round with the judges' eyes turned to you as the aggressor and then you end off each round the very same way, you could win the fight in a much more compelling way.

As an aside, returning to my point about commentators, I love to listen and learn from the learned words of the boxing anchors as they relay the nuances of the fight as they unfold. Sometimes when the final punch statistics are displayed at the very end of the fight, the commentators don't fully explain what lies beneath the fact that the numbers were not all that went on within the outcome. There might have been additional aspects such as who scored the more punishing punches. In addition, for those bouts where the outcome was more difficult to understand, look for who stole rounds and then keep in mind that the recency effect might well have been at play. Few are the boxers that close each round intelligently, but then again, few are the boxers that really think about what really lies behind the stealing of rounds.

USING YOUR MINUTE'S RECOVERY

The minute in between rounds of boxing is either spent or misspent depending on the organization of the corner and also your focus as the central member of that corner. If you carefully observe even the most experienced professional boxers, only some use their minute's reprieve wisely, where others move to the next round without much recovery. As you will see from what follows, the choice of how you choose to spend the critical moment in between each round is yours to determine. My obvious suggestion is that you work with your corner staff wisely to ensure you gain the biggest bang for your dollar, so to speak.

After a full three minutes of executing your plan you need to come back to the corner with a few objectives in mind. On one level you need to physically recover. What I mean is that you need to lower your heart rate, lower your respiration and also rehydrate so that you restore the water weight lost in sweat through the last round. Physically, the decision to do all of the above might not be fully visible in between Round One and Round Two. However, as you go deeper into the fight, the small effective decisions you too earlier will serve as a long-term advantage. Remember that good decisions earlier show up later on in the fight.

You need to also recover and re-focus at the psychological and emotional levels. Mentally speaking, you need to understand your experiences from the last round and what sorts of strategies and combinations are working versus not working for you. Remember that adapting to the challenges in the fight is all about understanding what sorts of results are materializing as a result of your efforts and also the efforts of your opponent. Obviously there is lots of information for you to bring back to your corner based upon what you have experienced first hand.

There are also aspects of the fight and how things are unfolding that can best be seen from the experienced observers on the sidelines, meaning your head coach and corner staff. These people will see things that you might not be noticing, only because you are in the thick of the action. Combined, you and your coaches need to exchange information very quickly and in a summary format so that you can take a few key things forward as you refine your plan and push your strategy forward in the heat of battle.

Having watched thousands of corners in action, I have noticed that the best corners have great communication, with that communication always following a common sense structure. The athlete returns to the corner, most often sits down, stretches his/her legs, takes a deep breath, swallows some water, all within the first 25 seconds or so. The next 20 seconds is about the exchange of information. Good coaches in the corner covey a few simple messages in the form of key words. Too much wording and explanation is usually lost on the boxer because of heightened respiration and heart rate. So, short and sweet is what works best. Within that information, suggestions have to be very specific. The coach who exclaims in frustration to "go and work harder" or "get busy" often is far too general. Coaches need to connect the dots with you. If you don't understand, then you need to ask. Understanding the how is what needs to happen in the exchange of information between coach and boxer within the crucial and tight timeline exchange.

As an aside, when things go well after a minute's rest, it is usually the result of good, solid communication in the previous minute's rest and recovery. In contrast, when athletes start falling apart in a bout, it is usually from a lack of connection between their effort and a successful outcome. Athletes on the downturn usually do not communicate well with their coaches just before their performances start to slide. The lesson that you need to keep in mind is that as an athlete, you must continue to communicate with your corner. That way, you and your coaches will be certain to remain on the same page. No matter what, keep the lines of communication open.

Finally, there is also the emotional recovery that I indicated was important at the very beginning of the last paragraph, above. Believe it or not, boxers win and lose their fights in part based upon emotions. Emotions are one of those double dividend categories where you gain or lose directly and also, indirectly. Directly, by feeling positive and charged, you become persistent and mentally tough. Sometimes the difference between a win and a loss comes down to emotions. The boxer who is willing to persist even when the odds are stacked against him can eventually overcome and succeed – I like to think of boxing in part as a war of wills. Willpower comes from emotions, and some people will themselves onto success where others sometimes choose to wilt. Notice I used the word "choose" to describe the differences of willpower when comparing two very different boxing outcomes – winning and losing in outcome. In relation to what needs to happen during the minute's rest, part of what has to happen is the re-building or refining of your emotional state. You need to come out of the corner with vigor and a building of positive momentum, and not a wilting that instead builds positive emotions like hope in your opponent. Hope is yours to maintain and also to build upon and guess what, as your hope and desire builds, not only do you feel it, so does your opponent!

PREPARING FOR WHEN THINGS GO BETTER THAN EXPECTED

When I worked in the amateur ranks as a sport consultant with a national boxing team, one of the senior coaches told me an interesting story from his days as a former amateur athlete and Olympian. What the coach shared with me remains at the forefront of my mind even today, almost fifteen years later. At the Olympics this coach – former athlete was preparing to fight a Mark Breland, an amazing athlete and superstar from the United States Olympic Boxing Team. There was no way that the Canadian athlete stood any chance of even coming close to his American opponent – the draw was a tough one and the Canadian boxer was in tough. As a consequence, he accepted the fact that this first bout was going to be his entire Olympic experience.

When the first bell signaled the start of the bout, the Canadian boxer did his best to keep up with the US boxer and to his surprise, connected with an amazing punch that sent Breland to the canvass. The Canadian boxer was so surprised that he couldn't find the neutral corner. In fact, neither boxer was prepared for this shocking event in the ring. With the precious seconds ticking away, the Canadian finally found the neutral corner, but his opportunity by then was spent. The opponent had enough time to recover and from that point onward in the bout, the US took the lead and went on to win the bout, and also the Olympic Gold Medal.

Sometimes we are faced with the best ever scenario without even having an adequate preparation for the opportunities that have arisen along with it. Opportunities like the one I have just described are experienced several times in every boxer's lifetime. Better than expected outcomes happen, but most of the time, we aren't prepared when we experience them. Though you might think that such monumental experiences are simply one off stories, I have been part of teams where my own clients have experienced very similar outcomes. Bottom line is that to be at your best you need to prepare for best scenarios, just as you prepare for worst scenarios.

When the opportunity taps you on the shoulder, it might be slightly different from a best scenario as you and your coach might have guessed it to be before the bout, but your response needs to be organized and sharp. You need to act when the opportunity arises and the opponent's jugular (so to speak) is exposed. You need to finish the scenario and for that to happen, you need to think on your feet. So, practice taking deep breaths during sparring and thinking quickly on your feet. Be one of the few who really decides to capitalize on your opportunities when they literally happen right in front of you.

CONTINGENCY PLANS AND RECOVERY

Just as some people let great moments pass them by, not responding to the opportunities they encounter, so too do boxers lose bouts they shouldn't have as a result of poor in the moment decisions. In sport psychology there is a large accumulation of research and literature about athlete coping. To cope essentially means to respond – react when an out of the ordinary experience results. As a boxer you need to be prepared for the best scenarios, though also all kinds of setbacks that need to be responded to effectively. Things don't always unfold as you see them in your mind's eye, even though the power of positive thinking does earn its rewards. The important thing in such cases is to respond with efficiency and intelligence when you get blindsided.

You need to develop contingency plans for the "what ifs" in boxing. The possible setbacks might be fighting with an injury, being a little off on the day of the fight, experiencing a flash knockdown, losing an important member of your support staff the night of the fight, and all kinds of other things that seem to come out of nowhere. You cannot predict or anticipate all of the possible challenges that you might encounter in the heat of battle. Just as Iron Mike once said, "everyone has a plan until he gets hit". I would say that his words are correct, but to them I would also chime in that some people actually do have backup plans for the times when plans go off course. I want you to be one of those sorts of athletes who are prepared for most everything encountered in the ring.

As I said, you cannot see every possible blip on the radar screen before it ever happens, and guess what, you shouldn't! What you do need to learn though, is how to respond to adversity. The scenario might be different than anticipated, but how you respond to setbacks should be somewhat standardized. Some boxers respond to flask knockdowns by getting to their feet much too quickly as opposed to using the allowed time for recovery. Other boxers press back into action much too soon after a low blow. Still others try to punch it out when they are exhausted, and all that needs to be done is a little bit of holding and some stalling for time.

As you can see, there are good and bad decisions that can be used in relation to each and every challenge. Though you might think that it is a matter of intelligence that determines who reacts wisely versus unwisely, you would be incorrect. Boxers need to rehearse in sparring how they should react in the split second where they face a critical challenge in their performance. The reality is that what you practice in training is most likely what will surface as your engrained habit, under pressure.

As an aside, I have learned through my own doctoral research that some athletes prepare for best ever scenarios and others are well rehearsed in terms of their contingency plans. You need to be well trained in relation to ideal and less than ideal events so that you can exploit both general types of scenarios to your best advantage, and not give up opportunities to your opponent. You will find that intelligent decisions in the moment of battle are the direct result of intelligent training – they are not innate.

KEEPING YOUR FOCUS DEEP INTO THE FIGHT

Not long ago I worked with a very skilled client. The client was fighting in a high profile bout against a very highly skilled opponent. The first three rounds went quite well for my client. He was pressing ahead and banking those early rounds, as he should have. At the end of the third round, the bell went to signal a return of the boxers to their respective corners. My client was extremely pleased with his performance and took his eyes off the opponent and started to turn his body, signaling that he was returning to his corner. With my client's back turned, the opponent took a chance and hit the back of my client's head.

On a related note, another boxer I know quite well recently fought against an important adversary while he was sharking his way up the boxing ranks. He knocked down his opponent early in the first round, turned his head, and slowly walked to the neutral corner. What do both of these athletes have in common? Well, both gave up their focus in a very important moment of their respective bouts. The first athlete, in being sloppy by taking his eyes off of his opponent allowed the opponent to get a shot in that should never have happened. The latter athlete was able to walk to the neutral corner without consequence.

The reality is that when you lose focus within a bout, sometimes there will be an immediate consequence, and sometimes there won't be. Regardless, you need to keep your focus within and across rounds, or at a certain point you will get caught! It may not be early in the fight when your reflexes are sharp, but you might pay the price later in the fight when you are slightly fatigued.

The topic of keeping your focus extends beyond the aforementioned example to another more general topic: the later - championship rounds. I am certain you can identify a bout you have witnessed where a boxer is doing great and slowly but surely he/she loses control of the bout and eventually loses as the result. Wins tend to sometimes slip away, but it doesn't happen all at once. Instead, a boxer becomes comfortable in his performance and becomes a little sloppy or uninspired. Mental discipline is an important asset that you need to carry with you from round to round, all the while reminding yourself that a bout is judged in its entirety and not just based upon good decisions early on. One of the commitments that my clients make is to perform to their highest capabilities from start to finish. Reminders are developed in the form of key words that help the boxer stay on track and committed throughout the complete performance.

Alternately, there are boxers out there today who are regarded as athletes that weaken in the later rounds. Why do such boxers fade? Is it solely a matter of their conditioning, or is there more to their fading than meets the eye? I would say that boxers learn to fade and eventually get caught out by a fighter who is more persistent. Then what happens is that the boxer loses confidence in his staying power. All told, the boxer then learns to fade and eventually regards himself as a fader. With his confidence and focus wavering deeper into the fight, the boxer eventually panics, gives up his control to the opponent, and the rest is history – literally. Bottom line: you need to re-commit to your plan ongoing, even when things are unfolding perfectly in the performance. By doing so you will keep the door closed to the opponent and he will be the person who wilts over time, not you.

FINAL REFLECTIONS

In this chapter we have looked very closely at what goes into performance from the first bell through to the final bell. There are all kinds of little pieces to the performance puzzle that happen before a performance but as I argue here, some focus and commitment also needs to happen in the performance itself. The topics we have covered off begin with the clearing of your mind before the first bell, proceed into the scouting out process within the first seconds to minutes of the bout, onward to stealing rounds through intelligent planning and tactics. Next, the reality is that you need to be prepared for best scenarios though also unforeseen situations that arise within a bout. For every ideal and less than ideal circumstance, there is an ideal and less than ideal response. Part of being a mentally tough performer is being prepared for most of what you will encounter, with well-rehearsed responses. You need to press and revisit your commitment to your performance through to the very end of the bout. Only once separated by the ring official should you allow your focus to soften and shift away from your opponent.

Combined, the aspects discussed in this chapter are essential to you becoming a complete – mentally tough boxer. There are no shortcuts to great performance. However, with the competition skills identified here, you can take a huge step forward, on your way to becoming that complete performer. Be prepared, be focused, and commit to a great performance within every moment of the bout. Your relentless focus will trump and surpass the skills that even an athletically superior boxer can throw at you. Finally, remember that you are not alone in the process of performance. You have a corner that is there for you to resource. Resource those people correctly, taken in their key suggestions, and then return your focus to the task in front of you, with even more focus.

Finally, remember that your performance has been built brick by prick, piece by piece. You have built a formidable mental game plan that started well before the bout and culminated in excellence within the bout. Even with an excellent performance, there will be places to improve. Be happy and enjoy the performance in the moment, but do not be fully satisfied with your comprehensive approach. Even in excellence there will be room for improvement. It is that improvement that will continue to spur you forward onto even better performance next time.

Chapter 13

POST-BOUT EVALUATIONS

Post-bout understanding is to me, perhaps one of the most essential topics for any boxer seeking to improve his/her mental game. We spoke considerably about how people learn and adapt in Chapters Seven, Eight and Nine. The importance of understanding to performance is critical and imperative. People need to understand where they came from in order to understand where they are going. Similarly, athletes need to understand their past and learn from it to really advance in a systematic way. Far too often, lessons are learned by athletes, only to be forgotten and then re-learned several months or years later on.

What gross inefficiency not to learn from mistakes. If we understand what works and doesn't work, why not go the next step and learn from it and then, push even further and integrate the lesson into athletic practices from that point onward? Believe it or not, much of my work is spent working very closely with boxers and their working teams, especially after bouts. The reason why is that I want my boxers to walk away from every performance with way more insight than they had walking into the bout. With more insight each time, you will be pushing your development forward and the basis of your understanding will indeed be built around facts and not fiction.

IMMEDIATE POST-BOUT DISCUSSIONS AND INTERVIEWS

So where should we begin? Well, the moment a bout ends we begin to make sense of the performance just completed. I have listened to many a professional boxer interviewed on HBO, immediately post-bout. Some of the responses are ones I like. I look for athletes who are able to connect the dots and explain how exact decisions taken during the bout transferred into performance, that in turn contributed to the end result of winning or losing. It is less important to me at this stage whether the athlete won or lost. Instead, I listen carefully to how and also, whether the boxer can make sense of the performance immediately after it is completed.

Mental restoration and recovery begins almost immediately after the bout has ended. I challenge you to listen to a few boxers who explain their performances on television just after their performances have ended. The explanations you will hear are perhaps the most authentic and heart felt explanations that any boxer will disclose. The reason why is that there is little time to bias explanations and delegate accountability through strategies that show the boxer in the best possible light. I look forward authentic words in all of my clients, and I assure you that with the experience fresh in the boxer's mind and no time to reason out who is responsible for what, a realistic explanation is always provided.

Some boxers will respond immediately after the bout with no explanation at all, especially after a loss. Others will provide some sort of vague response for the near win or large loss. Still others such as a Carl Froch are able to provide the sorts of precise explanations that I really like to hear. I am not going to name names of those athletes who provide the weaker responses, but I will tell you that more often than not, such athletes are less likely to recover from their recent performance and build understanding, that is unless they are challenged by a strong and focused working team. As an aside, every boxer who wishes to stay at the top of the game for a long time has to be willing to be challenged by his/her working team, but we will re-visit that discussion shortly.

MEETING AS A TEAM THE NEXT MORNING: STAGE ONE

The debriefing continues the following morning, almost immediately after the bout. I find that there are things about the performance that must be understood and documented on paper almost right away when the minute details of the day's lead-up and the performance are fresh in the boxer's mind, though also the collective minds of the working team members. When working with teams in debriefing the following morning and also during times where the team disbanded and was pulled together a few days later, I have noticed that the morning after has worked best for stage one debriefing. What do I mean by stage one debriefing? Well, the minute details that need to be understood in stage one include the minute parts of the bout day's schedule and how these were regarded by the boxer and team, how the schedule worked out from depart to the bout venue through to the entry into the ring and onward to the first bell, how equipment felt while in battle, the specifics about the exchange between the athlete and the corner, and minute things like that.

I have found that the logistical / procedural parts of the day of performance are remembered with accuracy the morning post-bout. They review of aspects in stage one should not turn to emotional discussions and rather, should only be about logistics and in terms of planning, how the system worked. You need to look for small details and pick up every little crumb in terms of things that worked out better in this recent bout versus all previous ones. You also need to identify the aspects that might have taken away from the overall quality of performance. Remember though, the focus in this stage one debrief is only to focus on procedural pieces of the puzzle and not the technical aspects of the performance.

The reason for a logistical debrief so early on is to remember details that otherwise would be lost a few days later. In sharp contrast, a focus on the technical aspects of the performance should happen any time from forty-eight hours later to five days, post-bout. As you and your team take some time and distance from the bout, certain pieces of your performance and also the performance of your team will become clearer. Clarity happens in terms of items that you were all emotionally invested in. So, my word of suggestions is not to rush to these pieces of discussion, even if every person is really wishing to tackle the technical and tactical parts of the performance immediately. You will not be ready to look at your performance objectively until at very least a few days after the fact.

For this stage one meeting and all other meetings that follow, identify one of the members of your working team as a note taker. You need to capture all of the pieces of the logistical feedback and eventually pull those details together as part of a larger post-bout report. Make certain that you are not the person serving as note taker and also make certain that all of the details are captured, not just the ones regarded as relevant to the person writing down the facts. If need ne, purchase an audio recorder and tape the meeting. If you do so, then you can take on the leadership role of drafting the eventual post-bout report when all of the facts are compiled.

FOLLOW-UP MEETINGS WITHIN THE WEEK: STAGE TWO

There are also more global – general evaluations of your performance that need to be considered once peoples' emotions are no longer invested in the result. Anytime from two to five days after the performance you and your team will find that the reasons for your result become much clearer. The insights that surround your performance will come in bits and pieces, and not all at once. As a result I always encourage boxers and their working team members to keep a sort of running list of their insights on a piece of paper. Remember that insights are often gained and lost when athletes and team members are not systematic, where they choose not to document the insights as they surface.

I will bet you of the 10 high profile boxers in the sport world today, at very least eight of these athlete fail to engage in writing down their insights as those insights come to the forefront of their mind. If you look at the long-term bout records of these athletes on BoxRec or any other website where records are readily available for all to see, you will find that even at the highest levels of the game, boxers are up and down in their results. The fluctuation in results is often times not a matter of being bested by a better opponent. Instead, many of the fluctuations in a boxer's record happen as a result of ongoing sloppiness and a lack of systematic insight, where lessons are learned and then integrated into the boxer's refined practices.

I challenge you and your team to be different than the norm. The task is an awkward one, but keep a pad of paper or notebook with you for the entire week post-bout. Another option is for you to use your wireless device and maintain notes as insights occur. Bottom line, you need to document, document, and document some more. Pick up every possible crumb that you can in the form of insights. I will show you what to do with what you have learned later in this chapter. Rest assured that the information does tie together into a systematic package, that can only enhance your knowledge, and from that knowledge, your bottom line capabilities.

Once the documenting has been worked on for up to five days, I always suggest that boxers and their working team meet once more. The focus obviously is mostly on the areas of discussion targeted after the stage one logistics meeting. I always suggest much like in stage one, that one person maintain notes or alternately, that the discussion be audio recorded so that all ideas and reflections are written down and captured.

The process for such a meeting is to start with the boxer, meaning you, and then to go around the room moving to coaching staff and then finally, sport science staff. Each person should bring his/her list to the meeting and cover off each point, perhaps delivering the information in a chronological sequence, starting with the insights in relation to further away from the fight and then moving progressively closer in time to the fight and finally, through the bout and post-bout.

Chances are there will be lots of repetition. Even if points are repeated by several team members, they are useful. If multiple people arrive at the very same conclusion, then you find consistency and the fact that people are in some cases on exactly the same page. In other instances, there will be aspects that will be unique to each member. Those points also are informative because they might shed some light on the performance from the vantage of each person's expertise. Bottom line: more information is always better than less information at this point. By actually going through this stage two debrief, you are already going considerably further than most every opponent you will encounter along the way.

THE POST-BOUT REPORT

Now comes the labor-intensive part of the process. You need to pull all of the information together into a document, either by computer or through writing out the details in summary format. I proceed is by developing a chronological report, with general categories. I start with a section with summary reflections from the last few fights, but I will return to what goes into the summary at the very end of this section. Next, I consider the pre-tournament general training. Within this second part of the report we consider your baseline fitness before you entered into a training camp or specific preparation for the bout. In addition, if there were any lingering questions about your mental game and your planning as experienced in the previous bout, they too are factored into the general preparatory section.

The section devoted to specific bout preparation targets all information that pertains to the tournament or opponent you have been preparing for. If you are an amateur boxer preparing for a national championship, you might consider the technical and tactical preparation in relation the specific opponents that you encountered during the tournament. Should you be a professional boxer, you would consider your targeted preparation in relation to the bout. For both levels of boxers, there should also be a consideration of how well informed they and their team were about the performance context, meaning the competition site. In addition, you will want to consider all tapering aspects that needed to be done for you to arrive in top shape. Finally, if there were any lingering physical, mental, and team-related questions that lingered from general preparation to specific preparation, and these questions were addressed or left untouched, they too should be documented in this section.

The next section of the report should be devoted to all aspects that fall within the week leading up to the fight. By then, you are no longer really in preparatory mode. Instead, you are likely tapering, making weight, resting, and preparing mentally for the fight and all of the specific implementation pieces that surround the week. If you found the week to be well organized, that you were well-rested, that the team pulled together, that the final training sessions helped you focus, that everyone around you helped enhance your performance, and that basically everything went according to plan or better, document those aspects and identify what you did that worked well during this critical stage of the performance. Remember, sometimes bouts are won and lost in the final week before the performance as a result of decisions compounded onto other decisions, for better or for worse.

If you find during the final week that you lost a lot of your time traveling from place to place and running around like a chicken with your head cut off, that too should be documented. You might also have noticed that some people around you took away form your energy, that you had trouble making weight, and that you final trainings did not sharpen you in relation to the performance(s) in front of you. There are many reasons why athletes look fatigued, over-whelmed or emotionally flat the week of the fight. Rest assured that such responses to fight week happen for a reason. The thing is to know why you gave up a little bit of your focus and energy so as to avoid that mistake going forward. The negative alternative to being critical of mistakes committed during fight week is to continue on making the same mistakes from one final week's preparation to the pre-preparation routine in advance of the bouts / tournaments that follow. Boxers can enter into a habit of under-achieving the week of the fight and wilting under the pressure. Though we discussed this phenomenon as part of Chapter Nine, the reason why people lose their confidence in the eleventh hour is due to poor planning, no learning, the re-committing of the same mistakes again, and then a lack of understanding in terms of why they continue to fall short. You need to be different and examine with magnifying glass precision the factors that explain fight week.

Next, look at the final twenty-four hours that come before the performance. Again, pull together all of the information related to this time frame in your performance preparation. Look very carefully at the events you did during this time, how you felt, what you did to fill your day, who surrounded you, and where the sequence of the day's plan contributed to a better performance and also where it detracted from the quality of performance you were looking for. Others will have provided you insight in relation to this time frame based on their observations seeing you at their different times throughout the day. Your coach will have interacted with you likely over, or just after breakfast. Your sport psychologist or motivational person (assuming you have one) might have seen you over breakfast, but also during a late morning or afternoon walk. Each person will have noticed things about you that were either tracking along perfectly, or instances where you looked a little off focus.

Next, pull together all of the facts surrounding the final three to four hours before the performance. Look at aspects such as nutrition and hydration. Did you during enough water? Did you eat food that sat well in your stomach and did you have your meal at the correct time in relation to the bout? Next, look at when you departed to the competition site and when you arrived. Did you have enough time to familiarize yourself with the environment and then proceed onward to the progressive parts of your warm-up. Alternately, did you spend too much time at the venue, without activities to build you focus. Then, did the structure of your warm-up leave you really sharp as you started your walk to the ring, or were you over-warmed or too cold? Next, were you able to build your sharpness in the final few minutes before the bout while you were entering the ring, touching gloves, and exchanging final words with your corner? You will have some reflections of how you felt and what you thought in these parts of your final bout warm-up. Your views will be supplemented by the observations of your working team. From the feedback, you should really gain a good understanding of how things unfolded in those last few hours in advance of the fight and most important, what aspects you learned for the next time around.

The second last section of the report should reflect all suggestions and discussions about the bout from first bell to the end result. Aspects that likely will surface during this part of the report will pertain to the technical, tactical, and psychological aspects surrounding the performance. Regardless of whether the feedback in this section is complimentary or critical of you and your working team, integrate in all of the information. Embrace what was said and do not leave out anything at all that could help you the next time around. There might feedback that you agree with and aspects that you don't fully endorse. Write in all pieces of the information from the meetings.

On the whole, you will always find at least a few crumbs and details that can be learned, even in bouts where you were exceptional and exceeded all expectations and your previous performance level. You need to look at these pieces of your performance regardless of what your result was and identify things you want to repeat and also, things you need to refine before you move forward and consider your next performance. Do not skip over this report without pulling in all of the details that were identified. Once you have the facts on paper, you will gain confidence from your systematic approach and from that approach, all of the insights you will gain.

BOXER-COACH FINAL POST-BOUT MEETING: STAGE THREE

The debriefing process should end with a final short meeting with those who you are closest to in your working team, though always, include your head coach. In advance of the scheduled meeting, provide the provisional report to the person(s) to attend. All of you should read the report and provide notes in the margins where wording is not fully accurate of what needs to be captured in terms of insights from the bout.

Next, during the meeting you can modify any aspects of the report that are slightly inaccurate. Then, together, you should pull out no more than one page of summary points that will eventually be repeated at the very end of the report. The summary points are the most critical things that need to be remembered and corrected going forward. These summary points will then be pasted to the beginning of the next fight's post-bout report because the lessons learned from the last fights should always inform the performance in the next fight. If you find that you forgot one of the summary points from the previous fight when you evaluate the fight that follows it, that too is important to note. Lessons should only be learned once and if necessary, only twice. Re-learning mistakes time and again is gross inefficiency and sloppiness, whereas the integrating of lessons represents profound efficiency and focus.

Once the document is corrected one last time and the summary points are added to the document, the exercise is concluded. You need to keep a copy of the report and provide a copy to the members of your working team for their information. Obviously the report will inform how each of you proceed as members of the working team as you all begin to fulfill your parts moving toward the next performance. Also, with the documented evidence from fight to fight, you should return from time to time and review the post-bout reports from previous fights, at very least to see how far you and your team have progressed. It is always amazing to look back and examine the facts as you acknowledge your steady and systematic progression as a boxer.

CLOSING THE LOOP – INTEGRATING LESSONS

Now that you have completed your fact-finding mission, you need to take what you know and press it into action. There is a distinct difference between knowing and doing – you need to transition beyond knowing to action! There is such a thing as being a student of the sport. Take for example Bernard Hopkins. There is no denying that Hopkins is a student of boxing. He thinks, eats, speaks, and lives the life of a boxer. Hopkins when he finally retires will be a first ballot Hall of Fame boxer. The basis of his success can be found in his fight record. Hopkins has ended many an amazing boxer's career. Have you ever wondered why Hopkins is so good and why he has stayed at the top of the sport for almost thirty years, where other big names have come and gone? The reason why can in part be witnessed in his column of Ring Magazine. What I respect most about Hopkins is his amazing – comprehensive approach to boxing.

I am presently working with a boxer who could be another Bernard Hopkins, if only he too chooses to close the loop and continue to grow and leaps and bounds. I cannot force my boxer to progress mentally, the choice is his to make. The decision he chooses will determine his longevity at the top of the sport of professional boxing. What needs to happen for this athlete is that he, also, choose to close the loop and integrate what he knows into his actions.

Just as it is the boxer's choice to either move forward through an integration of what has been learned, or not, you will also be faced with the same option. My hope is that you will always see the bouts in your pathway as loops with the lessons from each bout informing and revising your evolution from one bout to the next. Learn what you need to learn and then move on to the next lesson. There will always be things to integrate. As Bernard Hopkins prepares for his next bout, even with fifty-six bouts on his side, he continues to learn, tweak his systematic approach, and then press his plan into action. So, continue to close the loop and refine your plan with each fight, don't just talk about development, promise development, and then end with empty words. Finish what you have started and in doing so, gain the understanding needed for real – solid confidence.

FINAL REFLECTIONS

As you can see there is lots to be learned from post-bout evaluations. My approach to post-bout evaluations is comprehensive and labor intensive. Most boxers and coaching staff will look at how I work and say: "this guy likes to work with paper". They would be right, I am a researcher by trade and I like to work through case studies. As I have told you from the very start, you are a boutique operation. What you do and how you work makes you unique from all other people on the planet. You will share similarities in style, tactics, physiology, and psychology with other comparable athletes. But, you cannot possibly be the same as any other boxer in all of the dimensions I have just provided.

From the nearly twenty years of experience I have gained working with elite boxers, I know with certainty that few really learn from their performances in the systematic way I am suggesting in this chapter. Most boxers do their work through intuition, ability, and rote training. Some are a little more detailed and engage sport science staff in the preparation for performance, but even then, few really are thorough and systematic to the degree I look for.

When I begin working with boxing clients, some shy away very quickly from the methodology I advocate, or they choose not to work with details. On the other hand, the very same mentally lazy boxers struggle to explain why they experience their road bumps along their boxing paths.

I am not an advocate of guesswork and for some people, I ask too much and push way too far. On the other hand, it is not easy to create top class boxers, and even more challenging to push these athletes while they are at the top to new heights. Nonetheless, pushing is my job and much of what I do is wrapped around the concepts found within this chapter.

Planning is essential, and with systematic planning and the ongoing evolution of your plan, you will develop into the finely tuned boxer that you should be. If you invest as much attention into your planning and re-planning as you do into your technical training, I promise you that your performance will reflect your investment. I challenge you to go where almost every other boxer will not go: into the details and petty details that will define excellence.

In closing off this chapter where we began it, and so, closing the loop on this topic, read and re-read the parts of this chapter before each time before you engage in them. Remind yourself all that goes into stage one and stage two debriefing, and also remember the details that must be captured and then documented as a result of that meeting. Then, bring your report to the central members of your working team and refine the product into its final state. Finally, share the information with your entire working team in document form and then go the next step and move forward to more intelligent action with each progressive performance.

Chapter 14

THE WARRIOR'S PATH

To this point in the book we have spoken about the technical and tactical pieces that serve as parts of a boxer's mental edge. What I have come to realize is that even with the above sport science pieces, there is still one core piece of the puzzle that cannot be taught. This pivotal aspect of the boxer's composition is found at his/her very core. I like to think of the innate part of a boxer as his "spirit".

I would bet that there is very little written about what I will discuss in this chapter, but I have found a few books generally devoted to the topic, including the work of Dan Milman. Essentially, every athlete has a core of character and value. I find that for boxers to be at their very best, they must look inward and realize that they have an internal compass. There are things we each know about ourselves, but forget about and ignore. These central parts of who we are need to be part of what we bring to training and competition.

I don't know with certainty about you, but I can say personally that when things go very wrong in my life, in hindsight, when I look back over the setback, I always realize that I abandoned part of myself just as things started to go terribly wrong. I see in many boxers who are about to slide downward that they behave in a way that is not true to their character. The boxer might be one way in general life and try to be an entirely other person as part of his boxing persona.

One boxer I have known from his amateur days turned professional some years ago and then started on what was a very promising career. The boxer was a contender, and maybe, could have become a world champion. The sad part of the story is that the boxer never materialized into a top class boxer. As a person, he was intelligent, kind, open-minded, and clean cut. When he returned home to his friends he became a troublemaker, he fought in bars almost weekly, and he tried to present himself as a tough, heavy metal sort of guy. When he walked to the ring, the boxer would have heavy metal music piped through the arena. I always observed with interest because I know (and so did the athlete) that the image he was projec

I never did work with the athlete above, and sadly, his boxing career is quickly coming to an end. The reason for his premature and limited development stems from his decision to be someone he really isn't. The personality you choose in boxing must match exactly with who you are as a person. I like to call such a behavior "congruence". Essentially, your personality should become part of who you are in the ring and also, how you form your tactics and technical strategies for each fight. If you are a kind and intelligent person that should come through during all media conferences, stare downs, and performances. Essentially you need to be yourself. Who you are is a warrior, but your warrior spirit must match with your personality.

KNOWING AND BEING YOU

So who are you? In psychology there is a body of literature that generally indicates most people as bringing multiple selves with them, dependent on which context they step into. It isn't that each person has multiple personalities, but rather that we each behave in certain ways dependent on those who surround us. Most people to some extent where multiple hats because they want to fit in – they become chameleons with language, facial expressions, clothing, and as a result, thinking that suits the current social environment.

Though you need to fit into many social contexts and flex a little bit as you engage in appropriate behaviors, you need to always stay centered and aware of exactly who you are. When people get caught in lies, it usually happens as a result of the telling of multiple stories and fabrications. When people tell the truth, they never get caught in a lie, simply because the truth is simple to remember and easy to recall.

On the other hand, when people share stories or act in certain ways that are not truly them, they become confused. From confusion comes a loss of confidence, likely because the athlete is no longer living in reality. The bottom line is that you are who you are and your behaviors must match with your personality. I have spoken about double dividends several times over the course of this book, and this topic is one more time where the benefits are several when you know who you are and then stay true to yourself. On one level you have inner peach, which contrasts with the nervousness that out of touch athletes typically display. Second, those around you see that you are at peace and for those who work with you, your consistency is setting and facilitative of team confidence. Stepping outside of your team to the opponent and his/her team, when the opposition sees that you and your team are settled and peaceful, that display will become unnerving.

One world-renowned professional boxer usually works in his tactics to push his opponent outside of himself. His objective is to catch his opponents in lies and then to forecast those lies to anyone who will listen, through press conferences and the media. By the time the boxer touches gloves with his opponent, most of the time, he has unsettled his opponent and the team that surrounds that opponent. From there, the bout becomes easy as he continues to lure his adversaries away from who they are, either into a street brawl, inside fighting, or boxing, dependent on who they typically are. He looks to take the athlete away from his personality and fight with tactics that do not match with their personalities. Because those tactics are foreign and incongruent with who they are, they begin to live a lie in the ring and then he catches them in that lie.

You need to know exactly who you are and bring yourself with you wherever you go. If you were to do so against a boxer like the one just described, he would be at a total loss. The reason why is that he is so focused on pulling others outside of their true self, that all he would be left with is himself and his team, where he is forced to look inward to the very core of himself. So, look inward and consider who you are.

There are no surprises; you know exactly what you are at the very core. If you are a peaceful warrior, then your tactics are to fight fire with water. If you are an emotional fighter with a hot temper, then you need to develop your plan, fueled by emotions and feelings that will propel you forward. If you are a thinking fighter, your tactics must be built as much as possible around logic as your form of tactical warfare. The person you are as a boxer, must match with who you are, generally. The thing about long-standing great boxers is they know who they are and they represent themselves exactly as they should. Today, a few of the consistent boxers that you should really watch and read about are Andre Ward, Carl Froch, and Lucien Bute. These three fighters are distinctly different, with the first being highly spiritual, the second being highly analytical, and the third being a consummate gentlemen and tactician. Though I personally only know one of these three boxers, all seem to be consistent in their self-representation. Through consistency, all three boxers have risen to the top of the sport, often times trumping even better talent. I suppose staying true to yourself is also a talent, so much so that the few who remain true to themselves excel for the simplest reason of being self-assured.

REMEMBERING YOUR ROOTS

We spend much of our time focusing on where we are going. Topics such as goal setting serve to motivate us and help us remain on a path that will take us to success. I like to think of life as a trajectory with a past, a present, and a future. When people focus on the future without looking at their past, they often times forge a path that is winding, instead of straight – meaning straight to the top.

We each come with a history that explains why we are the way we are, and so, why we perform the way we perform. We have roots, a history, and so a beginning. I will bet that you started boxing for a very distinct reason. When I watched "Tyson" not long ago, it became clear that he was attracted to boxing as an alternative –adaptive behavior, meant to replace a life where he was on the street, and engaging in various sorts of crime. His roots traced back to Cus D'amato, who served as his mentor, his guardian, his alter ego, and his hope for a better life. So long as Iron Mike worked with this amazing coach, he performed at an exceptional level, and his behaviors matched with his personality. When his coach passed away, it seemed that Tyson began losing himself in a world of opulence, where he seemed utterly confused with who he should be.

In another part of my life, I work on Aboriginal (North American Indian) reserves with community members and youth. When I meet to work on a new research project with a few of the adults, they sometimes speak of having lost their way and forgotten their cultural identity in their youth. They continue on that they eventually have returned to who they are as adults and not engage in mentoring with present day Aboriginal youth. My colleagues are now adults, and many speak of having squandered their youth as a result of losing track of their roots. I suppose an old saying applied: "youth is lost on the young".

What I am asking you to do is something that most of your fellow athletes do not engage in and each day give at least a few minutes of consideration to where you came from. You are on a journey as an athlete and as a person. You started in boxing for a very distinct reason. So, what brought you to the sport? You need to remember when you started and related, how you were when you started.

There is such a thing as a "beginner's mind". You need to approach your boxing with a beginner's mind each day. The enjoyment associated with your first steps and moves as a boxer have to remain. Boxing is fun, and so is all of the sweat and hardship that you experience along the way. The counterpoint to a beginner's mind is the boxer who always walks into the gym exhausted and emotionally flat. During Chapter Five I spoke about the importance of training deliberately and with conviction. If you think back to the attitude you had when you started boxing, I will bet that you were enthusiastic. Chances are you couldn't wait to get to the gym and start working with your coach.

Each day is another opportunity gained or lost in terms of enthusiasm. When you remember where you came from as a boxer, you also remember why you are boxing today. You are not simply boxing because there is no other alternative. Some boxers at a certain point begin believing that boxing is all they have and that there is no other alternative for them – they feel trapped. Athletes imprison themselves and they also can release themselves from purgatory. The important thing to remember is that each day is another opportunity to return to your roots and retrace the true meaning of boxing, for you.

LIVING THE PART

The life of the long-term successful boxer is highly disciplined and focused. He/she gears life in relation to physical, psychological, and spiritual growth through boxing and through life. As I have said all along, life and sport decisions are banked and invested, and eventually you receive their dividends. If you live well, eat well, train well, have stable relationships, and focus your energy in one direction, you will outlast much better boxers.

Far too often, I witness boxers heading down the path to a shortened career. Some of the telltale signs of incorrect life focus might include excessive alcohol, carousing/promiscuity, excessive spending, and a focus on luxury items that are beyond one's needs. Ballooning in weight as a result of a lack of dietary discipline also shortens the lifespan of the aspiring boxer. If you watch the profile of boxers on HBO in the lead up to important bouts, you can find many a high quality boxer who exhibits some of the misspent life focus that I have just described. These athletes are great athletes, and in many instances, their days at the top are numbered.

There seems to be a belief in boxing that luxury items is the sign of success, and I understand why. Perhaps the athlete needs to have those sorts of items to paint the picture of success. Not long ago I traveled to a training camp where an athlete drove around in a rented car that was worth several hundred thousand dollars. The athlete took great pride in looking every part, a champion. My concern watching him was on what he was prioritizing during that training camp, and also, what he wasn't focusing on as the priority – focusing exclusively on the opponent and the upcoming bout.

I know for a fact that it is extremely hard for athletes to give up on appearance and instead, travel the road few travel. It takes outstanding focus and self-assurance to focus exclusively on training and the bout ahead. When athletes hunker down and focus entirely on training, they most often exceed all expectation. The reason why, at least in part, is because their opponent still remains invested in image and all kinds of things that really hold no value in terms of bottom line success.

Living the part means focusing only on what is important. Each step of the way there will be crossroads to consider. If you choose to go down a crossroad, it is a nice side trip, but at the same time it slows your overall journey to the end destination of success and excellence. As I have said once already, youth is often wasted on the young. The reason for this old - wise saying is that many talented young people waste away their opportunities on things that really provide them with nothing tangible as an endgame. Living the life of a boxer means that you commit to things that at the gut level you know are good for you. Other distractions that are "wants" should not be confused with "needs". What you need to do is focus and commit on performance and the things that take you closer to that performance.

STUDENT OF THE GAME

The reality of being a boxer, is that the very best ones from those at the top of the game live, eat, sleep, and speak boxing. To be a great boxer, you need to have a thorough understanding of your sport, more so than the boxers you are going to meet along the way. For some years I traveled with a national boxing team, while I was really learning the ropes about elite level boxing. Over the span of about eight years, the preferred style for amateur boxing changed several times from defensive, to offensive, now back to defensive style boxing. Each preferred style required that the boxers of that time adapt their styles and learn what exactly was needed to win tournaments, bank success, gain confidence, and qualify for the really big tournaments.

I have come to learn that often, the best boxers don't ever make it to the top due to a lack of understanding of what is really needed to succeed. I have spoken about athlete adaptation at length much earlier on in this book and have referred you back to Chapter Eight a few times. The reality in boxing is that to be the best you need to be intelligent, and I don't mean just the innate intelligence that you were born with. Instead, I am talking about the sort of intelligence that develops from really learning about what is needed in order to make it to the very top of the sport and then stay there.

When I worked with that amateur boxing team at one specific tournament, I noticed that my team's athletes were being eliminated prematurely despite the fact that often, they were the busier athletes. I never insert myself into coaching tactics as I am not a boxing coach, and I was never a boxer, either. However, the mistakes being committed by these boxers reflected a lack of understanding in terms of exactly where in the ring to land their scoring blows so that the majority of judges could see those blows land. In addition, the very same boxers were being landed on in geographic locations within the ring where the blows of their opponents were being scored by the judges. So, what was the difference between the athletes I worked with and some of the opposing national teams? The answer was that the better tactically prepared teams were using the ring to their advantage, whereas some of even the more talented boxers were being eliminated from the tournament due to incorrect ring use.

Boxers need to be students of the game and really understand how to go about working intelligently. I love to watch the outstanding high quality bouts featured today on HBO and ShowTime. Both of these networks bring outstanding quality bouts to the public. Within each bout, you need to move beyond just watching the match-up of styles and look much deeper into what is going on beneath the surface. Watch shows like 24/7 and you will gain access into the boxers' lives in advance of the bout. Pay attention to what they are saying, what their emotional expressions look like, whether they are dropping their weight correctly, whether they are surrounded by a supportive working team, whether they look rested, whether the glimpses of training look targeted and efficient, among a list of aspects that you could come up with. You need to look and examine those boxers and their lives much more closely than the average boxer does. To be a student of the game, you need to really understand what is going within and around the context as boxers prepare for better and worse performances.

The reality is that many boxers cruise their way through boxing careers and years of schooling with much less to show for their efforts than they should have. I am an advocate of old school effort and a blue-collar work ethics in the gym. I am also an advocate of looking, listening, and sensing what is going on with the boxers you meet along the way. I wise coach once told me that the average athlete learns from the lessons he/she experiences. Hopefully those lessons are learned efficiently so that they don't need to be learned and re-learned over and over again. The intelligent student of the game learns, not only from personal experience, but also by observing those in the surrounding environment. I suggest that you even go one step further and learn from the boxers you watch in higher profile bouts. There is a lot to learn and you don't have to learn everything from the school of hard knocks.

INNER PEACE AND STABILITY

Athletes also determine their success by many things that happen within and outside of the ring, based upon a factor that I regard as "stability". I am a fan of long-term relationships in life, because from time invested in a relationship, people learn the details about what makes their friend tick. There are certain things about you that are not at all technical. There is such a thing as contextual knowledge. Recently I listed to an unnamed boxing commentator explain why boxers leave their coaches and move on to new coaches. He explained that sometimes a change of face is necessary to refresh the athlete. I partially agree with what that commentator said – sometimes relationships become stale between coach and athlete.

On the other hand, I have witnessed athletes who change coaching staff and then end up performing well below their capacities, even when the new coach is a well-known authority in the sport. The reality is that coaches and athletes forge friendships and they get to know the inner workings of each other, so much so that they eventually are able to work like a hand and glove. They sometimes work together so well, to the point where there is no saying where the coach ends and the athlete begins (and vice versa).

Some unnamed highly talented athletes move from one coach to the next and never really develop a relationship with any coach. When you dig beneath the surface of those sorts of athletes, you see people who lack trust. On the other hand, how could transient athletes ever build a trusting relationship without any long-term history? The coach – athlete relationship is not an easy relationship, even among the very best of partnerships. There are arguments, coarse words that sometimes are not taken back, and many mistakes on the parts of both people. Though boxers, much like most any other athlete, need to find coaches who could develop them to the next level, I believe that sometimes, relationships are ended as athletes seek to trade upward to a bigger name coach. On the other hand, you will find that among the athletes with staying power and the highest level of consistency, many have remained with their coaches for long periods of time in order to build that hand – glove relationship needed at the very top.

When we think about stability, the discussion also must move beyond the athlete – coach relationship, to your relationships with other people in your life. I find that in elite sport, some athletes change their partners and friends regularly, especially their partners. In fact, I know of high profile boxers who move from one personal relationship to another at about the same pace as some unnamed famous actors. These athletes find themselves in and out of love regularly. With the fluidity of relationships, comes the responsibility of building a new tie, and getting to know a new person and her/his family and friends, both of which reflect parts of a major life change. With large life changes come ongoing adjustments in one's personal life and the stress that goes along with it. When these life changes happen at the very same time while you are preparing for an important fight, I believe that you can land up losing part of your focus to your personal life.

The thing is that for sport performance to be at its best, you need to focus on that performance with all of your being. I have heard athletes say that no matter what goes on in their life, that when it comes to boxing, they can go into their bubble and focus. In fact, some boxers live their life in constant turmoil, with some of that turmoil coming from changes in personal relationships. I do not believe that even the most talented athletes can perform at their best while their personal life is on the rocks and in decline. A tidy life allows you to focus on boxing because you have the peace of mind that everything else in your life is quiet and in harmony. There is something to be said about stability. It might not be the most exciting – daily experience in your life, but it is predictable, caring, and peaceful. As I said earlier focus is much like a pie, metaphorically speaking. You can only investment up to 100% of the pie in aspects of your life. To invest more of your focus in boxing, you need to have much more peace and tranquility in other parts of your life.

HANGING UP THE GLOVES

Given that we are quickly coming to the end of the book there must be a short section devoted to hanging up the gloves. I recall when I was an elite athlete that I hated hearing any mention about my future beyond athletics. Your athletic identity is likely a very big part of who you are as an overall person. Regardless of where you are in terms of your boxing development, there will come a time where you will indeed hang up the gloves, one way or another. The trick is to know when your natural time is to hang up the gloves so that you could turn your attention, either to coaching, education, another profession, and other life priorities.

As you well know, in the history of boxing, there are athletes who've overstayed their welcome to the point where their endings in the sport were sad, though predictable. Boxing is not one of those sports that you age gracefully in. I agree that there are a few exceptions to the rule, but even those athletes who perform into their forties at a certain point lose their speed and then their power. These athletes become a shell of what they originally were as they attempt to maintain themselves in the sport, beyond when they should have.

Personally, I remember working with one of my earliest success stories in professional boxing. The boxer, in his youth, developed into one of the amazing rags to riches stories on the international boxing scene. At a certain point I no longer worked with the boxer, though I did follow the latter part of his career with interest. Not long ago, the boxer fought against a much younger opponent who was physically strong and tough. The picture of my former client after the bout was sad. Even in his eyes the athlete looked sad and discouraged. He was not any resemblance to the boxer I knew several years earlier.

The goal is to know when the right time is to hang up the gloves and as you are starting to get a sense that the end of athletics is near, start looking for a substitute activity. The new activity is meant to help shift your focus from one part of your life into a new part of your life. As you know, life changes each of us and we need to adapt to the changes in our body as we move along. I am no longer an athlete, but I have become a sport psychology professor and researcher, though also a motivational coach.

You also need to develop a life plan that allows you to gracefully age out of athletics and onward to something new and exciting. Many a great coach was former elite athlete. Coaches such as Freddie Roach and Eddie Mustafa are perfect cases in point, and there are many other good examples, also. You can shift at a certain point to mentoring athletes, you could become a sport scientist like me, or you might wish to become a manager or boxing promoter. Finally, you might also wish to take what you have learned in sport to an entirely other field, such as business, law, or teaching. The choice is yours to make and the objective is for you to make the choice personally and not have boxing make that choice on your behalf.

GIVING BACK

Boxing is to me, the most profound sport. The level of friendships that are forged with teammates, coaches, and friends in boxing are among the most meaningful I have ever witnessed in the world of sport. Not long ago, I was traveling home after a consulting trip and the person beside me started talking. As the topic wandered onto boxing, the person in the seat directly in front of me swiveled his head around and joined the discussion. As it turns out, he was a Canadian Olympian from the sport of boxing. We started exchanging names and he gave me updates of athletes who became coaches or went on to other professions. It seemed that this former boxer was up to date with most, if not all of his teammates.

As we went deeper into this three-way discussion, one thing really hit home with me. All of the former boxers mentioned were in some way tied to boxing, even to present day, nearly thirty years after their athletic careers ended. Though some boxers step away from the sport at a certain point and move onward to other parts of their life, it is always inspiring to hear stories about those who give back in one way or another to their sport.

I will bet that as an athlete you have taken a considerable amount from boxing. Coaches and teammates are amongst the most generous people out there. These people give of their time and knowledge without any hesitation. As an athlete, you take that knowledge and build yourself up. There comes a point when a considerable amount of knowledge is banked as part of your boxing education. When boxers move on without giving back to their sport, lots of expertise and valuable experience is lost from the sport.

Working with the Canadian Aboriginal community I have come to learn that everything gifted to you is never really yours to keep to yourself. Gifts, like expertise, are to be passed from one generation to the next generation. In returning to the sport what you have borrowed from it, you complete the knowledge cycle and you also set a great example for the next generation of boxers.

In the section above, I also spoke about hanging up the gloves. Giving back through coaching, sport science, management, or a related area, also keeps the world of boxing within your grasp, though with opportunities that reflect your revised status as a former athlete and ongoing student of the sport. So, instead of aging out of the sport, you simply age out of one role in the sport and you look for other related opportunities that can be equally rewarding.

FINAL REFLECTIONS

Discussions about t path of the warrior are much wider discussions than any topics that have been written before the present chapter. Though I speak about life path and a more general philosophical approach as the second to last topic in this book, without it, all of the skills that I have raised reduce in their importance. You need to take a healthy and positive approach to boxing and also your life!

In this chapter, I have challenged you to look at your boxing as a part of your life, and not as the entire package. To be a great boxer, you need to first know who you are as a person. Who you are as a person must match with who you are in the ring. By having these two pieces match perfectly, you will be perfectly at home with your performance strategies and the underlying philosophy that you bring to the ring. Next, you do need to live the life of a boxer. That means taking good care of your body and your mind. If you live large out of the ring, your lifestyle will eventually surface in the ring and you will end up under performing at a certain point. Make small choices each day that take you closer to performance.

Part of your decision to live as a boxer should include becoming a committed student of the sport. I have told you all about boxers who were talented to the highest level and still fell short when it came to important tournaments. As you would agree, the most physically gifted athlete does not necessarily become the champion. Instead, the person who makes it over the long term is the person who gains intelligence and insight about boxing. Boxing is a game and it works by rules. Those rules at a certain point need to be integrated – they cannot be sidestepped. Instead of being one of those athletes who watches less talented athletes pass you by, why not become one of those boxers who through intelligence, passes by more physically gifted opponents?

To really immerse in boxing though, you need to have a tidy and clean life outside of sport. Your life organization outside of sport is going to follow you into the ring. If your energy is diffused through a complicated lifestyle with lots of partners, regular changes in coaches and friends, and over-luxurious and extravagant life decisions, your performance will eventually suffer – rest assured. What you do outside of the ring will eventually morph into who you become in the ring.

The rest of what was discussed in the chapter addressed a very delicate topic: life after sport. Whether you are close or far away from that point in your boxing career, there will come a time when you will arrive at this final topic. Preparing for life after sport is a necessary aspect of your athletic development. If you are just starting off in boxing, now is not the time to really engage in the discussion of life after sport. However, if you are past the mid-way point in your athletics, you need to start working on a transition away from athletics. Hopefully that transition will include a sharing if what you have learned from the world of boxing with developing boxers. I am always a strong advocate of closing the loop and giving what you have taken.

In closing, boxing is part of life and not the other way around. If you make the right choices for you as a person, those decisions can only enhance your performance in the ring. Dare to be different most other boxers and follow the true path of the warrior and all that it includes.

Chapter 15

CLOSING THE LOOP

As we come to the closing words of this book, chances are that you are flooded with all kinds of reflections and questions. In terms of the reflections, there is much to think about and do as you seek the mental edge in boxing. I have shared with you in this book some of my approach to mental training. No doubt some of my words were repetitious and matched with exactly how you and your working team go about training and performance. Other sections that I spelled out for you are likely new ideas for you to consider.

The goal is not to do everything all at once. It is virtually impossible to master every skill written about in this book, all at the same time. The person who tries to do it all from the very beginning will struggle. Your mind, like your body, is an amazing tool. It is a sponge that soaks in all kinds of important lessons that influence how you think and what you do as a result of your thinking. The objective is to channel the energy in your mind and direct it toward positive solutions, effective strategies, and adaptive responses to challenge.

If you look back to the opening two chapters of this book, especially Chapter Two, you will find that I asked several general questions and then tried to answer each one. In reality, we live our lives by asking lots of questions, and the questions never stop. You have to continue asking questions and searching for solutions, proactively throughout your boxing career. So, what follow are two very important questions that I think can close the loop in terms of this book.

WHERE DO I GO NOW?

The skills provided in this book are extensive, built from my experiences and observations working and watching some of the best boxers out there, today. As I watch each and every one of them, I can tell that at a given point in his/her career, the boxer has focused on furthering a particular skill. Some boxers return to resilience and mental toughness, others work on their adaptation skills, and still others focus on a blue-collar work ethic during training. The point is that each and every boxer continues to learn, re-works the skills we have discussed, and continues to grow in small increments.

The boxer who sits back after a resounding success and then rests on that success makes a significant mistake. As an athlete, you need to continue to move forward, and not to stand still. I have witnessed too many athletes, who after a great performance are so satisfied with their result, they start to believe that great performances will always be "in the bag". Great performance is not a given that will always be there for you. You need to always chip away at excellence. The important objective is to constantly move forward and also, to recognize what your developments are. The minute you stand still in sport you will be surpassed by someone else, including eventual opponents.

What you need to do is to read each and every chapter in this book. Some will be more important to you now, and others will become more important at certain times in your development as a boxer. Obviously, return to specific chapters when you need them! However, do not read this book, set it on a shelf, and let it accumulate dust. Instead, wear this book down and make it work for you. Touch base and read chapters as you need them, but also work proactively. Read sections and topics before you really need them with urgency. With time on your hands you will have the opportunity to really absorb the information and bend that information to you. I have spoken often about the importance of long-term studying, much like a good student studies several days in advance of an important exam. Similarly, you need to learn the information cold before it really counts.

So, balance your reading and read a must read chapter and also a chapter you want to read out of interest. By reading using the balanced approach I have just suggested, you will be in part proactive and part reactive. Your adaptation and evolution as a boxer will be safely developed as you continue to protect and also develop parts of yourself through a commitment to learning about the mental edge.

Am I Alone in this Project?

The responsibility of sharpening your mental edge needs a commitment by you and also by members of your working team. Starting with you, I have already indicated very early on in Chapter Seven that there is a tendency among all people to take the responsibility and bask in the sunlight when things go exactly according to plan. It is normal to feel good about yourself when everything goes right. When life deviates from what we predicted and we experience speed bumps and letdowns, the general tendency is to point the finger everywhere else but me.

Your responsibility is to work on you as best you can. If you don't commit to your mental edge, how possibly could you expect others to commit? You are the leader when it comes to your mental edge. You need to tackle the topic regularly and chip away at the tools highlighted in this book. The topics are conceptual I nature, but I also provide examples of boxers I've come across or observed along the way. You need to take all of the content I have shared with you and think: "how does this apply in relation to me?" You need to connect the concepts with your reality and every day existence. Go beyond reading the information and learning it to a level where you work on absorbing it.

Initially, you will find that you need to learn the concepts and become familiar with how each concept works. With time, you need to try the concepts and adapt them so that they fit you like a good suit or a good boxing glove. The application and refinement of the skills is your responsibility to lead.

However, I have tried to work with athletes on their mental edge, in cases where the coaches didn't support and integrate the work in training and performance. In those instances my work has failed. I no longer work with athletes, without also ensuring that their coaches integrate the concepts each and every day. The reality is that you need to learn and know the concepts, and the people who work with you in your environment need to ensure that your mental edge is a major focus in their application.

The people who need to support you with your mental edge include your coach, massage therapist, nutritionist, sport psychology consultant, and even your family members. All of these people influence you indirectly. What I hope for is a training and living environment where people close the loop and re-enforce what you are working on through this book. You do not train and live in isolation. People influence you for better and for worse. If you craft a supportive environment where people are up to date with what you are working on, you can then go to the next level and explore with each resource how they can contribute to your boutique operation.

ENDING WHERE I BEGAN

There comes a point when you need to put down this book and begin the "doing" part. If you didn't know them before, you now know the pieces that tie into the development of a great –complete mental edge. Few boxers really give full and detailed thought regarding how to build a solid mental edge from top to bottom. Even fewer systematically tackle each skill outlined and described in this book. The fewest still, meaning hardly any boxers go the distance and develop a comprehensive mental game plan and work each day to push their mental game plan to the next level.

The athletes who really do the mental edge work are few and far between, and personally, from those I know and observe from a distance, I can count such athletes on less than one hand. What makes these athletes special might be their physical talent, but then again, there are lots of physically gifted boxers in the amateur and professional ranks. What I believe makes the less than one handful of boxers at the very top who they are is a relentless focus on defining and refining their mental game each and every day.

The challenge I am waving in front of you starts and ends with your commitment, though also the commitment of your working team. What I challenge you to do is follow through where others stall out, for whatever excuses they come up with. You need to be different and walk an entirely different path than the average boxer. You need to know yourself, what makes you tick, and why. Then, you need to apply what you know each day.

Excellence is measured is small steps and not huge bounding leaps. Take small steps forward each and every day, and before you know it, you will surpass all expectations and become all that you are capable of becoming within the ring. The rest is up to you!

INDEX

D

E

F

target, 2, 3, 17, 23, 30, 34, 52, 73, 100, 114
taxis, 109
team members, 39, 48, 50, 53, 54, 55, 72, 85, 86, 112, 128, 129, 130
teams, 17, 48, 50, 52, 55, 67, 68, 69, 74, 75, 90, 99, 106, 109, 110, 122, 127, 128, 139
techniques, 69, 70, 85
teeth, 16
telephone, 107
television coverage, 119
television stations, 2
tension, 41
testing, 81
therapist, 22, 147
thoughts, 58, 60, 62
threats, 93
time frame, 33, 131
toys, 59
trade, 60, 133, 140
training, 1, 4, 7, 8, 12, 13, 14, 15, 16, 17, 18, 19, 20, 23, 24, 25, 27, 28, 29, 30, 34, 35, 37, 38, 39, 40, 41, 42, 43, 44, 45, 46, 47, 49, 50, 53, 54, 57, 58, 59, 60, 62, 69, 70, 74, 75, 76, 79, 88, 89, 92, 93, 99, 100, 103, 104, 105, 109, 113, 118, 123, 130, 133, 134, 135, 138, 139, 145, 146, 147
trajectory, 33, 137
transparency, 49
transportation, 109
tuff, 106

U

United States, 11, 33, 48, 122
universities, 11
US Basketball Team, 48

V

variables, 23
venue, 13, 23, 63, 72, 82, 109, 110, 112, 118, 128, 131
victims, 30
videos, 69, 93, 96
vision, 16, 25, 27, 28, 29, 40
visualization, 71
vocabulary, 59

W

waiver, 81
waking, 39
walking, 16, 20, 39, 40, 60, 63, 73, 80, 87, 88, 94, 108, 127
war, 21, 122
waste, 1, 35, 70, 76, 138
watches, 143
water, 71, 87, 121, 131, 136
weakness, 92, 96, 119
wealth, 10, 99
wear, 41, 81, 109, 146
web, 12, 45, 69, 93, 99, 111
websites, 14
work ethic, 28, 58, 140, 145
working conditions, 75
worldwide, 2, 93
worry, 44, 71

Y

young people, 138